VENTURE MOM

Garfield County Libraries
Parachute Branch Library
244 Grand Valley Way
Parachute, CO 81635
(970) 285-9870 • Fax (970) 285-7477
www.GCPLD.org

VENTURE
MOM

from idea to income in just 12 weeks

HOLLY HURD

AMACOM

AMERICAN MANAGEMENT ASSOCIATION

New York • Atlanta • Brussels • Chicago • Mexico City • San Francisco
Shanghai • Tokyo • Toronto • Washington, D.C.

This publication is designed to provide accurate and authoritative information in regard to the subject matter covered. It is sold with the understanding that the publisher is not engaged in rendering legal, accounting, or other professional service. If legal advice or other expert assistance is required, the services of a competent professional person should be sought.

LIBRARY OF CONGRESS CATALOGING-IN-PUBLICATION DATA
Hurd, Holly.
Venture mom : from idea to income in just 12 weeks / Holly Hurd.
pages cm
Includes bibliographical references and index.
ISBN 978-0-8144-3638-7 (pbk.) -- ISBN 0-8144-3638-2 (pbk.) -- ISBN 978-0-8144-3639-4
(ebook) 1. New business enterprises. 2. Businesswomen. 3. Working mothers. 4. Entrepreneurship.
I. Title.
HD62.5.H874 2015
658.1'1--dc23   2015002545

About AMA
American Management Association (www.amanet.org) is a world leader in talent development, advancing the skills of individuals to drive business success. Our mission is to support the goals of individuals and organizations through a complete range of products and services, including classroom and virtual seminars, webcasts, webinars, podcasts, conferences, corporate and government solutions, business books, and research. AMA's approach to improving performance combines experiential learning—learning through doing—with opportunities for ongoing professional growth at every step of one's career journey.

Printing number

10 9 8 7 6 5 4 3 2 1

CONTENTS

ACKNOWLEDGMENTS

When you tell your circle of friends and family that you are going to do something like start a business or write a book, you get many sideways glances. But you soldier on with your passion and work to make it happen, asking for help along the way. Writing this book has not been a solo project. Thanks to my entire team: the people at Amacom, my agent Joelle Delbourgo, and my editors Debbie Posner, Ann Beaton, and Marianne Wallace. Thanks to my darling husband who never gives me any doubt when I tell him the crazy idea that is my next project. And thanks to my wonderful children, Dylan, Waverly, and Chelsea, who support their mom through it all. I couldn't have done it without my wire fox terrier Luna who sits right behind me on my desk chair providing encouragement and company.

Finally, with great gratitude, I dedicate this book to my Dad, who always told me that I can do anything I set my mind to.

PREFACE

Are you a mom with an idea for a business? Do you make something so unique or outstanding that others want you to make it for them? Do you do something really well that others ask you to do for them? Are you in a job that you're really not happy with and find yourself looking for more fulfillment through your own business? Does the thought of starting your own business seem overwhelming?

No business plan, no start-up capital, no babysitter . . . no problem. Go from idea to income, from mom to venture mom, in only 12 weeks—and this book will help you get there.

I believe that most women currently do something in their lives that can be turned into a moneymaking venture and that it can be done in 12 weeks or less. If you are a mom who has an idea you want to turn into a business, this book will guide you through the process. In the course of 12 weeks, I will show you how to hone your idea, do just enough research to get started, come up with a cool name that sells, and market the idea or product to your target audience.

I will demystify the start-up process and make it simple and easy to follow. There are no complicated business plans. There is almost never a need to raise capital. I've interviewed hundreds of moms who started businesses without a business plan or a loan, not even from family or spouse. The 12-week program is structured so that you can accomplish a task each week that will take you closer to getting your first sale.

Venture Mom: From Idea to Income in Just 12 Weeks gives you concrete examples of successful ventures in a range of categories. By learning how other women have found success, you'll learn how you can, too. The book covers all areas of interest: food, fashion, art, children's classes, products and clothing for babies and children, animal-related ventures, Web and media ventures, and everything in between. Each success story in the first 12 chapters illustrates key points on the path to success, not simply the end result. These stories all have kernels of information that serve to both instruct and inspire.

When people ask why I started my website and wrote this book, I can point to two reasons: I love motivational books, and I get really antsy on long car rides. When my children were young, we rented a rundown ski house about four hours from home with some other families. It was on the weekly car rides to Vermont that *Venture Mom* was born.

I decided to come up with my own top 10 ways to stay motivated and fulfilled. When I looked around, the happiest women I could find were the ones who had created business ventures around something they loved to do. This resonated with my own experience: when I have a project, I'm on top of the world. I began to interview these women and write their stories. They were so compelling that, rather than wait to get a book published, I wanted to share their experiences right away. So I started a website and newsletter and called it what I was, a mom with a venture: VentureMom.

The paths to a successful venture were similar in so many aspects of the stories I heard that I developed a plan around what I learned from talking with these women. I'm a no-nonsense type of person, and showing other moms who wanted ventures how easily they could get started became the subject of this book.

I also learned that fear can be a huge roadblock. When I first started my newsletter, it took me two weeks to hit the send button. Knowing that this is a universal feeling can help new entrepreneurs overcome their own fear and get started on their ventures.

The timing is right. Women-owned businesses are thriving as important economic contributors in the U.S. and abroad. Between 1997 and 2013, the number of women-owned firms grew at one and a half times the national average, according to the American Express OPEN State of Women-Owned Businesses Report for 2013 (http://cwb.uschamber.com/women-entrepreneurship).

Many of the topics in this book could be (and have been) the subjects of entire books, but that kind of in-depth exploration is not the purpose of the 12-week program. This book aims to give you enough information—and inspiration—so you can move forward quickly and confidently.

INTRODUCTION

FIVE COMMONALITIES

There are five things all moms with successful ventures have in common:

#1. They have an existing talent, skill, or passion. First and foremost, most of these moms start a business around a passion that's already in their lives. It's usually a hobby that they love to pursue or a product they make that gets lots of compliments. Whether it's getting babies to sleep, remodeling bathrooms, or organizing pantries; whether it's making a great carrot cake, a beautiful necklace, or fabulous pillows, everyone has something they do really well, something that wins praise from friends and family. You've heard the expression "Do what you love, and the money will follow." It's true for most moms who have their own ventures. What is it that you do in your life now that you love to do and others need?

#2. They have a network of supportive friends and family. Friends and family always play a huge part in these stories. When you have an idea, tell everyone you know and get input, suggestions, and feedback. Someone always knows someone who can help you in some way. Successful entrepreneurs are not afraid to ask for help, and they spread the word on what they need. What is your idea and who can help you make it happen?

#3. They usually have no formal business plan. Most successful moms with their own ventures do not create a business plan. Most don't even have something written on the back of a napkin. Many women just seem to fall into their business ventures, whether they plan to or not. A friend asks for help organizing a closet. Or an aunt begs them to make a soup and salad for her bridge group. Or a neighbor loves the belt her friend created and asks her to make one for her. When this happens, these moms become aware that they have something that not only their friends and family would like and would pay for, but others might, too. But rather than take time to create a business plan, these moms just get started.

#4. They raise no start-up capital. Most successful Venture Moms start their venture without any start-up capital or loans. If some capital is needed they self-fund their ventures, usually with less than $500. Many get started by sending an email to everyone they know, telling of their service or product, and use initial proceeds to fund their venture.

#5. They overcome their fear. Finally, most successful moms are scared to get started. Many worry, saying, "What will my friends think? What will they say?" But many know in their hearts that their idea is something they must pursue even if they fail. It is common for entrepreneurs to have a visceral feeling that they must put their idea out in the world. You are not alone if you feel this way.

HOW THIS BOOK WILL HELP YOU

This book will help you succeed. By following the steps and assignments outlined each week you will be able to overcome the fear you may feel at getting started. You don't want to be sitting in your rocking chair 30 years from now, thinking about that great business idea you wish you had tried.

The book is organized into four parts. Here's how it works.

Parts I Through III

For the next 12 weeks, your weekly goal will be to complete the assignments described in each week's chapter.

It doesn't have to be perfect. As women, we strive for perfection and may seek the exact color orange for our logo or the perfect weight of paper for our business cards. My belief is that it's better to get started with something you may not be 100 percent happy with than to not get started at all. Remember, others don't know that you think the orange in your logo is too bright, or not bright enough, or not quite the shade you had in mind. They just see the success of your business. Focus on the big picture, and the details will fall into place.

Not to worry if you get sidetracked with life and you can't complete the assigned task for the week. Just hit reset and start again the next week. The goal of the book is to give you a stress-free program for starting a business venture. So if you miss a week, give yourself a pass and start again.

Part I, Figure Out What You Want To Do, focuses on what can be the hardest part—deciding what to do. This section can be difficult if you have literally no idea what interests you; but working through the assignments will help you figure it out. Chapters 1 through 3 will help you get focused. You must come up with something by the end of Week 3, even if you think it's not 100 percent right. (Many Moms start down one path and end up with the venture they are meant to have by just getting started with something in the general area.)

Part II, Get Organized, will help you do just that. Chapters 4 through 7 show you that it doesn't have to be perfect; it just has to be done. Pricing is key; you don't want to put something out into the marketplace without a reasonable price. This section will make sure you have a great name, a pricing structure, the start of a brand, and a website.

Part III, Put It Out There, takes you through the process of marketing your venture and setting up the framework for your marketing plan going forward. Chapters 8 through 12 cover the main aspects of marketing, from email campaigns to social media to networking.

Remember, the goal is 12 weeks, but you can alter the timetable if life gets in the way—and face it, it probably will. Some ventures will require more than a week to complete the tasks assigned. That is okay too, as long as you are moving forward. Many times you can continue with the next week while completing the thing that requires more time.

Part IV

Part IV, Venture Paths to Success, starts in Chapter 13 with a look at how moms can manage their lives with children while running a business venture. You'll focus on ways to manage your time to get it all (well, almost all) done. In Chapters 14 through 21 you'll find success stories grouped by area of interest. Read them all, even when they're not in your area of interest. There are always bits of very useful information found in other moms' stories.

This book will help you launch your venture in only 12 weeks. From idea to income, that is your goal. Are you ready? Here we go.

I

FIGURE OUT WHAT
YOU WANT TO DO

one

Week 1:
Discover Your Venture

Leslie Josel had no plans to start a business that would help organize life for children with ADD. But when her son was diagnosed, she read everything she could on the subject and discovered that kids with ADD do better when their world is organized. She started with organizing her son's room and then the entire house, creating systems for each task throughout the day. When Leslie told other moms how it had helped her son, they asked her to systematize and organize their homes as well. And because they were willing to pay her, Leslie had a business venture. Without any plans to start a business, she had solved a problem in her family and one that other families wanted solved too. Leslie calls her venture Order Out of Chaos.

Let's get started. This is your week for self-exploration. It's time to examine what really makes you happy and figure out what you love to do or what you already do that you're really good at. Like Leslie, you may be poised to launch a business you hadn't planned. You just have to realize that you have a potential venture and get organized.

Begin your venture journey by getting a notebook to record ideas, notes, answers to assignments, and everything you think of along the way.

Each chapter contains assignments to help guide you toward your venture. Work to complete the assignments during that week so at the end of 12 weeks your business is up and running. Use your notebook to record answers and complete the assigned tasks each week. Try to complete each week's tasks on schedule. If you find you can't, give yourself another week. Remember, this is about finding work you love, not adding stress to your life.

WEEK 1 ASSIGNMENTS

To guide you through the process of self-exploration, you have eight assignments to complete during Week 1. Even if you know what your venture is, I encourage you to complete all the assignments. They might lead you in a slightly different direction or help you to create something to enhance your current idea.

Assignment #1: Track Your Time

Keep a time journal for the week in your Notebook so you can see where your day goes and how your week lays out. Record whether you spent your time on work (inside or outside your home), exercise, errands and chores, with friends, with children and family, or working on a hobby. At the end of the week analyze where your time went. Tally the hours spent in each area. Take a good look at the hours that aren't devoted to routine tasks. What are you doing when you are the happiest? Who are you with when you feel fulfilled? Where do you like to spend the most time?

If you're thinking, "Ugh, I don't want to track my time," do it anyway. Remember, you're looking for time that you can carve out for your new venture. At the end of the week you'll be surprised how you spend your time and may realize that with just a few adjustments, you'll have more time for yourself, your family, and your venture.

 IN YOUR NOTEBOOK

- Record your activities for each waking hour of Week 1.
- Tally the time spent in each area.
- Analyze how you're spending your time on nonroutine tasks.

Assignment #2: Perform Imaginary Introductions

Imagine how a friend would introduce you when she wants to tell others what you do or what you're good at. "This is my friend, and _____." How would she fill in the blank? Here are some examples:

> "She makes the coolest jewelry."
> "Her oatmeal cookies are the best I've ever had."
> "She plans the most inventive kids' birthday parties."
> "She helped me choose colors for my whole house."
> "The photos she takes could be in an art gallery."
> "Her gardens are beautiful, and I wish she'd plan and plant a garden for me."

 IN YOUR NOTEBOOK

Imagine how the following people would fill in the blanks: "This is my _____ (who you are to that person) and she _____ (your talent or skill)." Record their imaginary introductions.

- Yourself
- A parent
- A friend
- A child
- A coworker
- A mate

Assignment #3: How Would You Spend Your Free Time?

Imagine you had an hour, a full day, or a week with no mommy commitments. You could do whatever you wanted with that time. What would you do? Would you go to the gym, take a yoga class, make a cake, plant a garden, take photos, or go shopping? What project would you work on? What hobby gives you immense joy? Write down how you would most like to spend free time.

 **IN YOUR NOTEBOOK**

What would you do without any other commitments?

- In an hour?
- For a full day?
- For a full week?

This week is for brainstorming about what you already do, what you love to do, and what your talents are. Gather your thoughts on what you might do. There are no limits. If your dream is to create a television cooking show or become a world-class exercise guru, take note of it. There may be a kernel of a venture in that idea. Dare to shoot for the moon.

Assignment #4: Collect Clippings, Take Notes

Gather your favorite magazines—travel, decorating, gardening, cooking, sports, whatever interests you—and add images to the thoughts you've recorded. Clip photos of things that make you happy, pictures of things that you want to do, photos of people, places, and things you like. Look through all kinds of magazines. Usually what you have around your home is what really interests you. Add these to your Notebook.

 IN YOUR NOTEBOOK

Make a list of the kinds of books, magazines, blogs, and websites you like to read. What do you watch on TV or read online? Do you turn to programs or sites on cooking, exercise, travel, public opinion? Record the answers in your Notebook. Make a note of what feeds your soul. This assignment is similar to creating a wish board, where you put all the things that you wish for in one place. When you look at the clippings and list of readings they should provide clues to your perfect venture.

Assignment #5: Get Your Ideas Flowing

Now, let's focus on the things you do very well and the activities that bring you joy.

IN YOUR NOTEBOOK

Answer the following questions:

* What did you love to do before you became a mother?
* Is there something you do or make that always gets complimented?
* What talent of yours do other people admire?
* What do you enjoy?
* When do you feel most fulfilled?
* What did you enjoy doing in college, high school, and grade school?
* What career intrigues you? What do you want to learn more about?
* What activity or hobby makes you feel energized?
* What do you admire? Who do you admire? Why?
* Was there a part-time job you had that you loved?
* What five things do you want to do before you are seventy-five?
* What would you attempt to do if you knew you would not fail?
* Is there something you love to do that you want to turn into a career?

Assignment #6: From a Different Perspective

Now we'll come at the question from another direction. In this assignment, you'll fill in the blanks to get a clearer picture of the things you love and the talents you have.

 IN YOUR NOTEBOOK

Complete the sentences below:

* I feel so great and energized when I' m _____.
* I've only done it a couple of times, but I love to _____.
* Everyone around me tells me I make a great _____and should sell it/them.
* When my friends need help with _____, they come to me.
* In a local talent show, my talent would be _____.
* If I were the star of a TV show, it would be about _____.

Now your creative juices should be flowing, your Notebook filling up, and new ideas germinating. There are no wrong answers, too few answers, or too many answers. During this week keep notes on what makes you happy, what you enjoy doing, what fulfills you, what energizes you, and what you can't get enough of.

Assignment #7: Determine the Goals for Your Venture

Think about your personal goals for your venture. The answers to these questions will help you structure what you do.

 IN YOUR NOTEBOOK

Answer the following five questions:

1. Do you want a part-time venture?
2. How many hours per week can you devote to your venture?
3. Is making a certain amount of money imperative?
4. Do you want something you can grow or take beyond your local area?
5. Do you want the satisfaction of creating a business?

Assignment #8: Where Does Your Happiness Come From?

Let's continue to narrow down the interests and activities that will define your venture.

 IN YOUR NOTEBOOK

In each of the questions below, number the options in order, with 1 being the top choice, 2 being your second choice, etc.

What do you love?

- ❑ Food
- ❑ Animals
- ❑ Home
- ❑ Garden

❑ Computers and Technology
❑ Fashion
❑ Health and Fitness
❑ The Arts

With whom, with what, or where would you like to spend your free time?

❑ In the kitchen
❑ At the dog park
❑ In a fabric, furniture, antique, or accessory store
❑ In your garden or at a gardening center
❑ At your computer or helping someone with their computer
❑ In a department store or fashion boutique
❑ In the gym or working out
❑ In a museum

Who or what would you rather be with?

❑ By yourself
❑ With animals
❑ With children
❑ With people

Is a pattern forming about what you like to do, where, and with whom? Do you prefer to be at home with your computer? Is your favorite place in a clothing boutique with friends? Does cooking for others make you the happiest? Is biking outdoors your go-to activity?

Look at your ratings and write down what your "thing" is.

SEE WHAT YOU'VE DISCOVERED

Now that you've completed these eight assignments, you have discovered quite a bit about where your talent lies and what you love to do. For example:

* You like to be outside.
* You like to be in front of a computer.
* You like to be with animals.

- You like to be with kids.
- You like to exercise.
- You like to cook.
- You like to travel.
- You like to write.
- You like to teach.
- You like to be with groups of people.

In your Notebook, summarize what kinds of activities make you happy, where those activities take place, and who you are with when you engage in them.

What do you already do that others would pay you for? All of this information will inform your venture decision. At the end of this week, look at what your notes and answers point to. A clear focus on a particular area should be developing.

DISCOVERING YOUR VENTURE SUCCESS STORIES

The stories that follow highlight the interplay of self-knowledge, talent, skills, and serendipity. I think you'll find them inspiring.

The Naptime Chef: Kelsey Banfield

She loved to cook, but when Kelsey Banfield's first baby was born her time in the kitchen became erratic at best. She found a way to incorporate her love of cooking with her newborn's schedule. When other moms begged Kelsey for her ideas and recipes, this turned into a venture that she had never planned.

When her hobby collided with her professional life it was an eye-opening experience. Kelsey Banfield was a self-professed foodie. In her first job with a large hospital, she found herself putting together a collection of recipes to create a charitable cookbook to benefit the hospital. As it was being compiled, Rizzoli Publishing jumped on board and the collection of recipes turned into a professionally produced cookbook. Kelsey's job was to see the book through the process from design to publication. Her first baby was born one month after the book hit the stores in 2007. Kelsey was not sure what her next career move would be, but she was sure that it would be in food.

Kelsey said, "Before my daughter was born my husband and I enjoyed our time cooking and eating. We had a blast trying out new recipes every week. And then we had a baby. My vision of maternity leave was me in the kitchen with a sleeping baby in the swing, whipping up dinner as usual. Boy, was I wrong about that."

Most moms call dinnertime the witching hour, when small children get cranky and need a lot of hands-on attention. Preparing a meal can be almost impossible. But Kelsey wanted to keep her cooking passion alive in her new life. So she decided to prep and assemble everything while her daughter napped in the afternoon, so that the meal would be ready to finish off at 6:00 P.M.

One evening as her playgroup was heading home to get takeout again, Kelsey pulled a homemade lasagna out of the oven as her husband walked in the door. The moms were stunned, saying, "When did you make that?" Kelsey's response was, "During naptime." Her mom friends dubbed her The Naptime Chef, and they wanted her secret.

With her friends clamoring for recipes and ideas for becoming naptime chefs themselves, Kelsey started a collection of recipes reworked to be prepared during naptime. She wondered if more moms might want the same mealtime solutions, so she decided to share her ideas through a blog she called The Naptime Chef.

Kelsey's blog audience grew right away and she was noticed by a popular parenting blog called Babble, which asked her to write for them. Before long The Naptime Chef was hitting the big leagues, writing about food, doing food product reviews, and, of course, providing busy new moms with great ideas for easy, healthy meals.

Soon an agent came calling and Kelsey was on her way to publishing her own book. "I have to pinch myself. This is so much fun and so rewarding to be able to do something I love." Kelsey's book *The Naptime Chef: Fitting Great Food into Family Life* hit bookstores in the spring of 2012. Now that her first book is done, Kelsey spends her time writing and testing recipes for future books. She even offers in-home cooking lessons.

Kelsey says, "This whole experience has confirmed for me that this is something I want to do forever." You can bet that there are a lot of moms out there making great meals during their kids' naptimes who would call Kelsey their hero.

TAKEAWAY

- Kelsey knew what her love was, food; where she wanted to be, in the kitchen; and what she wanted to be doing, cooking.
- Kelsey started a collection of her recipes on a blog with no start-up capital after her friends pointed out a talent that she had that they could use.
- By looking at how she spent her time each day she was able to see how she could carve out time to pursue what she loved.

Smart Playrooms: Karri Bowen-Poole and Chris Simpson

When these two moms transformed a playroom for a friend using ideas that had worked for them during their days as preschool teachers, they fell into a venture. Karri and Chris were both teachers who saw the need to create play stations in home playrooms just like those found in schools. After transforming her sister's playroom, Karri saw an idea for a business venture and asked Chris to join her to expand her territory.

Sometimes helping your family can lead to a venture. When Karri's sister lamented that she had just finished renovating her playroom but her kids never used it, Karri came to the rescue. She had been a teacher for 20 years and was trained in how to engage kids in play. She spent the day creating active play stations in her sister's playroom just like she had for her students. Karri organized the toys and games in bins and labeled them so the kids knew where everything was stored. After the transformation, Karri's sister said, "It's amazing, my kids love it. They're in the new playroom all the time, and they even clean up."

After hearing about her sister's experience, other moms asked Karri to help them redo their playrooms. Karri realized she had uncovered a need that wasn't being met. Systematizing what she did for her sister, she developed a format to follow for creating others. Karri named her venture Smart Playrooms. Initially clients came from her Westchester County community, but when her longtime friend Chris Simpson moved to Connecticut, Karri saw an opportunity to expand. Chris had been a special education and elementary school teacher in California and had complementary skills, so the two became a team. "It's more fun to work with someone, and we get ideas from each other. And when one of us has a kid issue, the other one can cover." The women are on call all the time, but because they work for themselves they are able to turn their phones off when they need to, returning client calls as needed. And now that their kids are older their available time to work and take on more projects is expanding.

Together, they can create a playroom from scratch or take what a family has and redo a playroom to provide educational and creative play areas. "We try to use as much as the family has in the space they have. We will recommend certain toys and give resources when needed."

Chris and Karri say, "Kids are so scheduled today, they need more time for playing on their own to help develop their executive functioning skills." One mom told Chris and Karri, "I could not have imagined that a day spent organizing toys could change my life. But it did. My kids now can find everything and play and clean up all on their own, even my eighteen-month-old."

Some moms ask them to help organize their homes as well, but Chris and Karri really like the idea of using their educational backgrounds to create play spaces that help kids grow. And this gives them a niche in the market. To market their venture, the two often give a Smart Playrooms redesign package to local charity auctions. "This has been great at getting the word out about what we do."

Chris and Karri love that they are able to use their past careers in their current venture. "Sometimes moms are skeptical, but when they see the transformation of their playrooms and see how their kids play in them, they become believers."

TAKEAWAY

- Karri and Chris used skills they already had to craft a venture.
- The two women saw a need that others would pay them to fill.
- Karri and Chris realized they liked working as a team and saw the benefit for their business.

eBay Storefront Fasta fa Zool: Janet King

When her parents died, Janet King had all of her parents' things to dispose of. Janet realized many of the things could be sold, but because she lived halfway across the country she boxed up the items and sent them to her own home. Janet decided she could create some income using a "garage sale" website to sell the items. It took only a few hours to learn how to use eBay and she was on her way.

With a large trove of unwanted treasures from her parents' house to dispose of, Janet King looked to eBay. When she began, Janet didn't even know how to get a digital photo on to her computer. But in a few hours, and with the help of several online tutorials, she taught herself, listed the items, and they sold.

Now she was hooked, and she began to search for other things to sell. "I learned that many people peruse eBay looking to replace china. People were looking for things like a Wedgewood teapot they broke or another six Noritake plates for an upcoming christening. Others were looking to add to their collections of things like Royal Doulton figurines or antique tin toys." Janet saw what sold and learned what things were worth in an online marketplace.

Janet also discovered that Hollywood set designers use eBay to find vintage items. So she set out to add additional items to her eBay store by haunting tag sales, thrift shops, and flea markets. Wherever she goes, she'll buy items she thinks she'll be able to resell. Janet's most famous find was a Cartier belt she bought for $1 at a tag sale. She sold that belt for $1,800 on eBay.

Setting up storage at home, Janet now has a basement lined with blue bins filled with these finds. Janet spends her time photographing the treasures and creating the detailed descriptions that will go in her eBay store Fasta fa Zool. (The name comes from her father's favorite saying, "fasta fa zool," meaning a little bit of this and a little bit of that—a play on the name of the Italian soup *pasta e fagiole*.) She's so busy, she's hired an assistant to help her—another mom looking for flexible hours. She won't consign items, preferring to pay a seller up front so the things are then hers to sell. She also spends time researching the value of pieces that she finds, a fun part of her day. Summer is her high season, with many families moving.

Since the downturn in the economy, people call her hoping to sell wedding gifts, such as full sets of china or Waterford crystal, which they find don't fit with the way they live today. She will then resell the items in her eBay storefront.

Janet feels this is a learning experience for her two boys, ages 17 and 14, who help with the business. And her husband helps with repairs when necessary. Setting daily, weekly, and monthly goals keeps her moving forward and hitting her target income. This is the first time she's been her own boss and she says it's the hardest she's ever worked. And she's taught several friends, other local moms, how to resell items on eBay. With lots of treasures available to change hands, there can never be too many sellers online.

TAKEAWAY

- Janet fell into this venture out of necessity.
- Janet enjoyed the search for items and the research into their value so much that she decided to make it a business.
- This is an easy business to start with very little outlay of cash or start-up time.

———

On to Week 2, when friends and family will help you refine your venture search.

two

Week 2:
Get Input from Friends and Family

When Leslie Pearlman missed a call from her pediatrician because her phone was in the bottom of her stroller bag, she lamented, "I wish there was something that would hold my phone on the stroller handle." Light bulb! If something like that didn't exist, then why not create it? She mentioned the idea to her husband, who told her that his uncle's friend was in the plastics business. Leslie reached out to him. He couldn't help—but had a friend who could. After creating a prototype, Leslie presold the newly named Texthook to small stores in her area before she even placed her first bulk order. The Texthook is now in baby stores everywhere. It fits most phones and can be used on exercise equipment as well. Family and friends helped her get there.

Who knows you better than your friends and family? And who else will help you more than they will? Get out your Notebook and start cataloguing ideas from your friends and family. Meet for coffee, make a phone call, send an email, grab dinner, have cocktails. Everyone loves to help a start-up business. Friends love to give advice on where your talents lie. Family can be your biggest fans. You'll be turning to this group frequently as you develop your venture, so be sure to spread goodwill by offering something in return for their time and support: Offer to cook dinner, treat for coffee or lunch, watch their kids, or gift them with your specialty. It's time to get some input and feedback.

WEEK 2 ASSIGNMENTS

Family and friends play a huge role in many mom-run businesses, and in many different ways. To help you tap your friends and family for ideas, encouragement, and honest feedback, here are your assignments during Week 2. Don't feel as if you are imposing. People love to be asked for advice and feedback.

Assignment #1: Tap Your Friends for Ideas

Ask at least 10 friends what they see you doing as a successful business owner. If you can't manage to meet with 10 friends or family members in the course of a week, meet with as many as you can. Listen closely and be ready to record what they say. Don't worry if their suggestions sound over the top or unattainable. You're still gathering ideas from which to develop a venture.

 IN YOUR NOTEBOOK

Meet with 10 people who know you well. Ask each friend or family member the following questions and take notes on their answers.

- What do I do well?
- What is one talent I have that I could put to work for you or for others?
- What can you see me doing for a venture?
- Is there something that I make or do that you covet and others would too?
- If you could see me succeeding at any job in the world, what would it be?
- What problem do you see me solving?
- If I were a famous business person, who would I be?

Craft some questions around your interests and talents.

- Everyone loves my spiced pecans. Do you think I can package and sell them?
- When people come over they always say they love my perennial gardens and want me to plant one at their house. Do you think I could set up a venture doing that?
- I love taking care of animals. Do you think there's a need for dog-sitting in town?

These kinds of questions may lead to answers like:

"You always get a delicious and healthy meal on the table. I wish you'd cook for me."

"Your necklace is so cool. You should sell those."

"I can see you coaching girl's lacrosse."

"You'd be a great French tutor."

"You always find the coolest home accessories."

"You're the best dresser. You should offer to style people or take them shopping."

"You are so great on the computer. Can you help me with social media?"

"You are so great with numbers, you should be a bookkeeper."

"You make the best carrot cake. You should sell it."

Within these answers you'll find your venture. Look at the responses and make a list of potential businesses. It may help to look at what other moms have created. See how other moms have gotten started with one sale or client and grown from there.

Look back at your notes from Week 1 about how you would like to spend your free time to see if your venture ideas gel with your venture goals. You need to look back at what makes you happy. If you admire the hours of your friend who has a dog-walking service but you don't like dogs, it's not your venture. If you need to make money but the thing that you create only sells for five dollars, can you grow that venture to get to the income level you need? Ask yourself how the venture idea fits your interests, your likes and dislikes, and your needs.

Assignment #2: Test Your Ideas

Test your ideas on at least 10 friends and family members. (Again, if your schedule keeps you from meeting with 10 people this week, meet with as many as you can.) This can be the same group you surveyed in Assignment #1, or a totally different crew. Ask them what they think about your venture ideas. Don't let naysayers get to you; when it's right you'll know it. Look at the answers from your friend interviews. Look at what you do well, what you already do in your life or what you love, and come up with more venture ideas. Look at what others do within your area of interest. It's there—you just have to see it.

Here are two examples:

You love to cook and have been told your seasoned pecans are great. In Assignment #1 when you ask friends and family for venture suggestions, you may hear someone say, "Your spiced nuts are awesome, I'd buy them." Then, in Assignment #2, you would ask, "I'm thinking about packaging and selling my spiced pecans. What do you think?"

Suppose you love planning your kids' birthday parties. In Assignment #1, a friend may say, "You plan the best children's birthday parties." In Assignment #2 you could ask, "What do you think about my starting a service that plans kids' birthday parties?"

You may have to lead your friends with questions like these:

"I love choosing paint colors for home décor. Would someone pay me to do that?"

"I'm great at putting together family trips to cool places. Would you read my blog if I started one on family travel?"

"You've had my ice cream cakes. Do you think local restaurants would carry them?"

"I love to tutor young kids in reading and have a teaching degree I'm not using. Do you think I could charge for private tutoring?"

"People always compliment me on my _____ (insert what you make). Do you think I could sell them in boutiques?"

 IN YOUR NOTEBOOK

Record the responses of friends and family to your ideas for a possible venture.

Assignment #3: Brainstorm

Get together with a group of four to eight friends and have a brainstorming session. Remember the basic rules: All ideas are welcome; no discussion, judgment, or criticism are allowed; and the goal is quantity over quality. The purpose is to generate all kinds of venture ideas for you, so open up the discussion to anything at all. Have fun. Write everything down, regardless of how silly or outlandish it may sound. The comment "You'd be a great Martha Stewart" may be funny, but perhaps when you look at it later, you may get other ideas. Take notes on everything you hear during your brainstorming session and record them in your Notebook.

One mom is thinking about starting a venture but doesn't know what direction to take. But she does know how to maintain her home. All of her friends tease her about how meticulous she is at having systems serviced and curtains cleaned on a regular basis. Who wouldn't love a book or reminder to do those things in their own home? She'd be just the person to outline that. So, she may not want to have an empire like Martha Stewart, but she could start a newsletter/reminder service to help people remember what needs to be done to keep their homes in top shape. While most of this information is easily found online, her knowledge of local vendors and her ability to customize her services for the local market are keys to how she can build her venture.

She could self-publish a small book with a yearly schedule of needed maintenance. She could give talks to local groups and become the guru on home repair and upkeep. She could list the local vendors she likes to use for curtain cleaning, rug stain-proofing, generator maintenance, basement systems, etc. She has lots of ideas on home maintenance that she assumes everyone knows but they don't.

As new vendors get started or old service companies slip up, she could update her followers. She could sell her booklet to real estate agents to give as gifts for their new home buyers. She could become the expert, go-to mom and consult with new homeowners who have never taken care of a home before—and charge for her time. There are endless ways to build a business around something that she does well. She just needs to package her talent, just like you can package yours.

Assignment #4: Zero In on Your Venture

So back to your task this week—getting ideas, input, and feedback from friends and family. At the end of the week take some time to look at all of your notes and start to zero in on what you think you'd find fulfilling based on what you love to do or you already do really well. Look at your notes and see if there is a kernel of an idea that has the potential to grow into a venture. Is there something that keeps coming up? Remember, the goal is to have a concrete venture idea by the end of Week 3. It doesn't have to be forever. Many moms start up one business path but end up doing something else. There is nothing wrong with trying several ideas.

 IN YOUR NOTEBOOK

Read over your notes from this week's meetings and conversations and make a list of possible ventures.

FRIENDS AND FAMILY SUCCESS STORIES

Given what you love to do or already do or have been told you do well, several ideas should be crystallizing. Read the following stories to see how other moms got started with guidance and input from friends and family.

Gramma Napoli's Marinara Sauce: Karen Schulz

Friends had told her for years that her marinara sauce was amazing and she should sell it. But it took one particular friend to get Karen Schulz to make it happen. That friend helped her get started and placed the first large order for jars of the sauce. Another friend helped with packaging. Their encouragement got Karen moving forward and into her business venture.

After leaving her event-planning job when her first baby was born, Karen Schulz knew she wanted to start her own business but wasn't sure what it would be. Over the next twelve years her house was always filled with kids. To feed this hungry group, Karen would smother spaghetti and meatballs with the sauce her Gramma Napoli had taught her to make. The kids gobbled it up, and their parents and Karen's friends always raved about it.

Gramma Napoli had been the gatekeeper of the secret family recipe for marinara sauce that her children and grandchildren had been enjoying for years. She eventually shared the sauce recipe with Karen, who still has the olive oil–stained yellow index card it was first written on. When Karen was 25, her Grandmother passed away, and Karen was left to carry on the tradition.

After all the encouragement she got from friends and family, Karen finally got serious. She talked to a friend who owns a gourmet food store in the town where she lives. She decided she wanted to sell Gramma Napoli's sauce at the local farmers' market but had no idea where to begin. Her friend June, of June and Ho Park's gourmet food shop, not only gave Karen advice but asked to carry the sauce in her store.

"June got me to cross that line in the sand," She was apprehensive, so June asked her to bring a sample to the store for a taste test. The sauce was a big hit, and Karen had her first order. For Karen this was a home run. Not only was June a savvy business woman, but the store, which caters to busy, choosy moms who want fresh, healthy food for their families, was a perfect fit for the sauce. Now Karen had to deliver.

Gearing up with jars and supplies, Karen asked a graphic designer friend to help with packaging. Her friend combined a favorite old photo of Gramma Napoli with Karen's tag line, "cooked with love," to create the label. Karen delivered her first dozen jars of Gramma Napoli's sauce to the gourmet store, June & Ho, in October 2010. With the enthusiastic support of friends and happy customers, the orders keep coming in.

Karen loves that her kids are seeing her pursue a business venture that she enjoys so much. "It's been very fluid and organic, how this happened." What's next for Karen and this delicious sauce? She's thinking about expanding to the Internet. Who knows? The whole country may soon be enjoying Gramma Napoli's secret sauce.

TAKEAWAY

- Karen's friends guided her to her venture.
- One friend with experience helped her figure out what the next steps were.
- Another friend helped with packaging so there was no outlay of cash for design.

By Hand Granola: Suzy McCarthy

Her son gave Suzy McCarthy the idea for creating a business around the granola she made for family and friends. He even put the business model together. Suzy's daughter crafted the packaging and logo. By Hand Granola is truly a family affair.

During a summer vacation, she tasted a fabulous granola at a local bakery and thought, "Why not create my own granola at home?" Over the course of the next year, Suzy McCarthy spent hours at bookstores poring over granola recipes. Searching out and tasting other blends gave her insight into what she wanted in her granola. Suzy and her high school daughter Kelly experimented until they finally hit upon a combination of ingredients that they loved.

Suzy kept the house stocked with their new snack for her family to enjoy. She also began wrapping it in cute cellophane packages to give to friends as birthday presents and hostess gifts. Their granola became a coveted item.

Then came a move to the West Coast. Suzy's son Whit, a recent college graduate, decided to head west with the family to look for a job. But he also had an idea for his mom. Recognizing a great product, Whit encouraged his mom to sell her granola, but Suzy resisted the idea of gearing up for a business. She had been in advertising prior to having kids and had run a successful women's boutique with a friend back East, but she balked at the idea of taking this on. A business selling granola seemed overwhelming. Whit promised to do everything related to the business side of things. With that support, Suzy took the plunge. She and Whit became certified to cook and sell a food product.

With her daughter there to help with a name and package design, making granola became a family venture. The name By Hand Granola and the logo are a clever play on the fact that the granola is made by hand to eat by hand.

Hitting the streets in December 2010, Suzy and Whit got their first order their first day out from a local gourmet food store. More stores followed and the work to make enough inventory became challenging. They found a commercial kitchen where they could prepare and package the growing number of orders. Suzy did the cooking, and Whit managed the vendor relationships and deliveries.

According to Suzy, the best part of working with her son was seeing his excitement and enthusiasm. And for him to see a business grow from an idea to a profitable venture was a thrill for both of them. Suzy and Whit's next step was working the Web—customers can now order their granola from anywhere. "I never thought we'd be doing this together. I love that I'm bonding with my son while managing a joint venture," Suzy says. Who knew her son would lead Suzy, *By* (the) *Hand*, into a venture for both of them?

TAKEAWAY

- Family stepped in to help get the venture going.
- While Suzy spent a long time developing her recipe, it only took a few weeks to figure out how to cook the granola in bulk, get the proper licensing to cook at home, come up with a name, and develop a package.

Artistic Photography: Barbara Erdmann

Often, it's your kids who lead you to a venture. Barbara Erdmann had been an avid photographer all her life, but family and friends encouraged her to make it a business.

When she walked into a kid's clothing store where she had been shopping for years, it struck Barbara Erdmann that the bare walls would be the perfect spot for some large-scale photos of kids—they would look great and be good for sales. She asked the manager if she could photograph her own kids and their friends in the clothes from the store and display them on the walls. The store manager loved the idea and said yes.

Photographing her children became her hobby, and that led to photographing other kids and families. But Barbara's eyes were always open to new opportunities to showcase her work. Her boys attended a large indoor sports arena, and again she had an idea. "I approached one of the owners and suggested that I photograph kids playing sports on the indoor fields and make them large-scale prints to line the walls of the entrance. He said yes and I had my second assignment."

Then her work took a different turn. "I began to take photos of nature and scenery on our family vacations," Focusing on horses in Colorado, sand in Turks and Caicos, and waves in Nantucket and Block Island, Barbara's eye for creative photography found new subject matter.

Once again, her kids led her to a defining moment. An extreme closeup of a chrysanthemum that had just come into bloom, taken on a trip with her children to the New York Botanical Gardens, brought her to a new stage in her venture. "The shot was incredible, showing layer upon layer of the petals. I hung it in my own home and when friends asked if they could have one, I knew I had a venture."

This is when Barbara sought help to achieve the kind of aesthetic she wanted in her photographs. A friend told her about Photographic Solutions in Norwalk, Connecticut, who guided Barbara on what paper to use for specific looks. "They have become part of my team and I work with a local shop that does all of my framing." Taking classes at Silvermine Art Guild, Barbara enhanced her skills and honed her craft along the way.

Armed with the confidence she gained from the feedback from friends and family, she went to a local home goods store and showed them her photographs. "They loved them and took several pieces right away to display in the store." Getting input from several mentors in the design business, Barbara worked to showcase her art. Through word of mouth, making lots of phone calls, developing her designer contacts, and making store visits, Barbara now has her work in five shops in the area and demand is growing.

What does her family think of her newfound venture? "They are proud but still want me to get dinner on the table." And how does she feel? "Finally I feel whole. I love my family, but this is not about anyone else making me feel good but me." And now Barbara's photos are making others feel good too.

TAKEAWAY

- Barbara began by putting her love of photography to good use with no plans for a venture.
- Friends introduced Barbara to her two primary sources for printing and framing.

———

This week you reached out to friends and family for ideas, feedback, and support. Next week, research will help you to crystallize your venture.

three

Week 3:
Do Your Research

When Abby Flanagan decided to turn her hobby of taking family photographs into a business, research was an important step. In the portrait area of her venture, she looked at two things: equipment and pricing. She found this information easily on the Web, at her local camera store, and through several informational interviews. She was also planning to take photos of homes for local real estate firms. Abby asked potential real estate clients what they required of the work.

When Abby turned her attention to photographing landscapes as art, she took a great deal of time figuring out how to achieve the look she wanted. Mounting her photos was a critical aspect of production that she needed to research as well. She visited the local photographic shop that she was considering for the job of printing and mounting her photos and talked with a specialist, getting options and pricing. All of this research helped Abby to develop her product and plan her venture.

This is an exciting week. By the end of Week 3, you should be ready to choose a business venture. Research will help you test your assumptions and finalize your choice. As in the example above, when Abby decided she would turn her love of photography into a business, she needed information, such as what equipment to use and what to charge. With each new project, Abby used research to guide her to a sale. What information do you need to make a decision on your venture?

By the beginning of this week you should have identified an area of interest, or something that you already do, that will be the basis of your venture. Week 3 is about research and exploration. To keep on track to make your first sale in 12 weeks, you'll want to come up with a venture by the end of this week. Keep notes on all of your research in your Notebook.

WEEK 3 ASSIGNMENTS

Knowledge will give you power, so concentrate this week on learning all you can. Some ventures may require more research than a week allows. Do as much as you can, but give yourself more time if you feel it's truly necessary.

Assignment #1: Start with the Internet

The Internet is an amazing tool that can arm you with all you need to know. Search the web and read everything you can about your area of interest. See who offers the service or product you want to provide. Who is doing exactly what you want to do or something close? Who is selling what you want to sell? How do they structure their service? What do they charge? Keep all relevant sites listed in your Notebook so you can revisit them.

 IN YOUR NOTEBOOK

Gather a list of at least ten ventures that are similar to what you want to offer. Make a chart or spreadsheet and use it to record the following information for each venture:

- Venture name
- Web address
- Service/product
- Price
- Target market
- Description
- Notes

Assignment #2: Look into Taking a Class

Here is where you may run into a time crunch. Because I want you to commit to a venture this week, taking a class may delay that decision. If you find a class that you feel will help you to develop your venture, read the course overview and talk to the professor or instructor to make sure it will fit your needs. You can move on to Week 4 while you take the class if that makes sense.

Is there a local school or library where you can take classes? Look for classes online as well. Perhaps you want to offer administrative services to businesses or individuals. Online classes can help you fill in areas where you need to enhance or upgrade your skills. Or maybe you need to acquire new software skills for your own venture. You can teach yourself how to use Excel, PowerPoint, Constant Contact, iContact, and countless other office applications online. Is your goal to start a business helping people set up websites? GoDaddy, Network Solutions, and many more website providers can help you get started.

One mom developed a business around helping older individuals learn to use email. Remember: something that comes easily to you may be extremely difficult for someone who's had no exposure to that skill. What about the entire business of organizing and presenting photographs? You can become an expert on a particular photo program and offer to make photo books. Many classes are offered at night (sometimes free) at local libraries and can be completed in just three hours. If you feel strongly that you could build a venture in this area but need to enhance your skills, a short class may be all you need to get started.

Maybe you love yoga or Pilates and want to offer your own classes or individual instruction. Several moms have started at the simple level and offered classes in their basements or at local venues, like senior centers or clubs. Research what certifications are required and begin your schooling. Get training to expand to more advanced techniques within your field. One mom started teaching simple Pilates and is now trained to teach on the reformer machine. She got training for the advanced area as she was offering the more simple techniques she was certified for. She didn't let her long-term goals stop her from getting started.

Let's look at the example of a mom who's a retired lawyer and wants to offer a legal service. While she probably won't need to take a class, she will need to find out everything she needs to know for the service she has in mind, which is to offer a package to entrepreneurs for trademarking their company names. Her assignment this week is to research everything about how to help others register for trademarks. She plans to do research online and at the library and to reach out to law firms and friends in the legal community to find out what's involved in preparing to file for trademarks. Much of what is required can be found on the actual site where you file.

Her professional background will make this process easier. She might even volunteer with a local firm or a lawyer who specializes in trademarks. If you choose something that you used to do, something you're doing as a hobby, or something you love, you probably already have a knowledge base from which to build a venture.

Find out if your venture requires any type of license or certification. If so, this may extend your timeline. In some areas of business you can get certified as you progress. If you are starting a food venture, check state and local regulations to see what is required in your area to sell food prepared at home. As part of your research go online and ask the question, "What is required to sell food cooked at home?" You should be able to find the information you need for your state or county.

Figure out whether you want or need to take any classes and sign up. But keep things simple. This shouldn't delay the start of your venture; rather, it should add to your expertise. Continue on to Week 4 if you can. Or, if you must, wait until you complete your class.

 IN YOUR NOTEBOOK

- List the classes you might need for your venture and where they are offered.
- List the pros and cons of taking a class at this time.
- Record any licensing or certification requirements for opening your business.

Assignment #3: Get an Informational Internship

Is there someone doing what you want to do who needs an extra set of hands? If you want to garner experience in being an event planner, offer your assistance on a particular job at no charge. If you have a food product you want to offer, reach out to women who sell cookies or granola in local stores. Ask them how they got started and how they grew and if you can see how they work and visit their production facility. Ask other mom entrepreneurs how they grew their ventures. What was their path? One mom I know was known for making decorative cookies for special events but wanted to expand into event planning. When she would get a call for cookies, she offered her event-planning services at no charge to establish this new area of her venture. By offering her services at no charge in the beginning stages, she was able to build a reputation in an area other than cookies.

See if you can shadow another woman who runs her own business for a day or two. Many businesses won't turn down an offer of free help. This is an excellent way to get hands-on experience in what you want to do.

 IN YOUR NOTEBOOK

* Gather names of local mom-owned businesses that might welcome free help for a day.
* Make a list of all possible internship opportunities in your area.

Assignment #4: Conduct Informational Interviews

Conduct at least two informational interviews with people who are doing what you want to do. Offer to buy them a coffee or bring coffee to their studio or home. Or talk with them by phone. This is a simple process. Email a contact telling them you'd like to chat with them about their business and just need about 15 minutes of their time. If a friend refers you to someone, be sure to mention the friend in the email. Ask them what time works best for them either by phone or in person.

Get together and ask them to tell you about their business. Prepare pertinent questions, such as how they got started and how they get clients. Other information, such as what they charge for their products or services, can usually be found on the Web. Do your research beforehand, and be mindful of the other person's time.

If you want to be a photographer of children, contact a local photographer and tell him or her that you're considering starting a business. Offer to assist with a shoot to see how they work and ask them what equipment and supplies they prefer to use and why. Find out who they use for developing and what they charge. If you can't sit in on a shoot, meet with them and ask about how their pricing works, what marketing they do, and who their target market is. Keep notes on everything you learn.

If you want to be a dog walker, talk to an experienced dog walker. Offer to go along for a morning of walking. Ask them where they get clients, what they charge per walk, how many dogs they walk, what times of day they are busiest, and how they organize their weeks.

People love to share with newcomers. Some people might view you as competition, and that's okay too. Be honest about wanting to go into the same business.

If you can't find anyone to interview in your town, reach out to someone in another town. Everyone does things in a different way and appeals to a different audience, so don't be discouraged if your town already has 15 children's photographers. You'll find a way to stand out and be unique.

 IN YOUR NOTEBOOK

- Keep detailed notes of each informational interview.
- Record your impressions: What did you learn that surprised you? What confirmed what you already knew?

Assignment #5: Tell Your Story

I love this exercise. It really helps you to zero in on how you see your venture taking shape. You'll need to choose a friend or two whose input you value and with whom you can be completely honest.

Ask your friend to tell an imaginary story about you and how your venture will develop. As you react to her details, you keep reshaping the story. Using the example introduced in Week 2, let's say you're a master at keeping your house together and maintaining your home's systems.

Your friend might say, "You're so great at keeping your house up, I see you starting a blog and then writing a book." Then you say, "I don't want to write a book, but might write a blog." She goes back to her story and starts over: "You write a blog and are approached by a well-known magazine to do a question-and-answer series for them." You say, "I don't want to do a question-and-answer series because I don't have enough experience yet." She starts again, "You write a column for a local newspaper and get enough followers to advertise on your blog." Together you keep reshaping the story until it's about a venture you can visualize yourself engaging in.

Craft a story that is tailored to your needs and fits with how you see your venture taking shape. Try to include a timeline and four or five steps you need to take to get started. For example, the friend says, "You can start a Facebook page about keeping your home up this week. Then, next week you can send an email to everyone you know and ask them to Like your Facebook page. The week after you can set up a blog," and so on. You can do this exercise with several friends and get multiple answers. Keep everything in your Notebook for reference later on.

Nothing is too outrageous. As the saying goes: "Shoot for the moon, you might hit the top of the fence." The friend may say, "I see you with your own TV show telling homeowners how to maintain their homes." You may not make it to NBC, but perhaps webinars are in your future.

Here's another example. Your friend says, "You make the best key lime pies. You should sell them to friends and family." You say, "That's not enough of a venture for me." Your friend says, "You could sell them to caterers for parties and make small bite-size ones for passing around." You say, "I want something bigger, maybe my own storefront." So your friend says, "You make other great pies, why not open a pie store with various kinds of pies?" You say, "No, I don't want to staff a shop, so what if I sold online and also offered a pickup out of my home? I think I want to stick to key lime pies." Your friend says, "Start with caterers, then restaurants, then reach out to Whole Foods and find out what their requirements are. Ask other vendors how they got into Whole Foods. You can rent a commercial kitchen and increase your production once you get sales." You may not make it nationally, but by finishing your story, you're forced to see the path.

By the end of this week, you should have done enough research to move on to Week 4, where you will name your venture. You'll need to choose your venture this week in order to move forward. Remember, it doesn't have to be perfect or what you plan to do forever. Many successful moms start out down one path and end up somewhere else. You may start out offering a home management blog and end up with a caretaking business. You should be open to change, but it's important to move forward. If you are truly stuck and feel you can't identify something you want to be doing, take more time. But keep reading, as your venture may come to you as you continue.

RESEARCH AND EXPLORE SUCCESS STORIES

The following stories show you how other moms have put research to work for their ventures. One had been doing research for years; another, well, after a failed attempt. And our third mom knew exactly who to turn to for help.

Bodha Skin: Brittany Chamberlin

Bodha Skin is a great example of creating a business venture around something that you have created for your own use. When Brittany Chamberlin couldn't find the kinds of products she wanted for her family, she developed her own.

Her time working for a nonprofit in the environmental field led her to her venture. As a professional, Brittany Chamberlin looked at the way toxins affect the environment in general, but when she started to understand how toxins affect individuals, she got a wake-up call. "I realized that what we put *on* our bodies is just as important as what we put *in* our bodies. Shockingly, many everyday beauty products go unregulated." Brittany felt that she wanted skin care products for herself and her children that were all natural.

By taking online courses and workshops, Brittany became deeply informed about developing basic skin care products, and she began to create her own whipped body butters and hand creams using ingredients sourced in the United States. "The first thing I created was a lavender face cream that was ultra rich for the winter months. I used it myself and gave it as gifts to friends and family." The cream was an instant hit and she realized she might be able to make a business out of her newfound passion.

Brittany read everything she could on nontoxic skin care, followed multiple blogs on the subject, and consulted with experts in the field. Through this research, she decided to get her product independently tested to confirm its environmentally safe status. And it was. All of Brittany's products are handcrafted and contain certified organic butters and exotic and essential oils.

To begin, Brittany supplied her body butters to a small test market to get feedback from potential customers. She chose the name "Bodha" because it is the Sanskrit word meaning knowledge and understanding. "My goal is to help customers understand the benefits of using chemical-free products for their entire family. I have learned that eighty percent of what we put on our skin can be absorbed into the bloodstream and the average woman applies ten to fifteen products per day."

Brittany began to sell her skin care line at farmers' markets, at craft fairs, and on the Web. She used social media to provide information to her customer base. The Bodha Skin line offers a range of products, from a body mousse (ideal for pregnant bellies) to hand salve to a body butter for babies.

Brittany is focusing on education through her blog and would love to see her line in stores everywhere. With a two-year-old and another child on the way, she is managing the growth of her small company but can foresee a future with her whipped body butters found in homes everywhere.

TAKEAWAY

- Brittany's desire to have access to nontoxic skin care products led her to create something unique for her family.
- The research for this product took months, rather than weeks, but while she was waiting for results, Brittany moved forward with naming and branding her line.

Romance Novelist: Jamie Beck

Readers can learn from how Jamie Beck worked backwards. She jumped in and then did her research. Jamie was challenged by a fellow writer to draft a romance novel. She did and it was structured all wrong. She found this out when she joined romance writers' groups and learned how to properly structure future novels.

When she was younger, she loved soap operas, and *When Harry Met Sally* was her favorite movie. But how did Jamie Beck turn her love of romantic stories into a new venture? In her previous life, she was a commercial real estate lawyer but left to raise her two children. And then, "When they started school, I became bored."

When Jamie really thought about what she loved to do, she had an interesting idea. "Always when I was on the treadmill exercising or waiting in my car at pickup, I would create stories in my mind and it was really fun. Or I would create different endings for movies." An avid reader of romantic books, she thought it might be fun to try to craft her own romance novel.

Jamie had taken a creative writing class in college and was corresponding with some writers online. "One friend bet me I couldn't write a novel. As my idea solidified, I set out to prove him wrong." When her kids were in school from eight to three, Jamie's obsession became writing a romance novel like the ones she loved to read.

It took about eight months to complete a coming-of-age story titled *Unexpected Song* and, "It sucked." Now what? "I came at this backwards," Jamie says of her decision to join writing groups and take classes *after* completing a manuscript. At the Connecticut chapter of The Romance Writers of America, Jamie found a sounding board and a lot of new friends. "I met such diverse people from all walks of life; it was a whole new experience. We get together for workshops and critique sessions." This involvement gave Jamie an inside look—and a framework, so her second manuscript (soon to be her debut novel) was better than her first.

With the completion of her third novel, which took second place in a writing contest, Jamie did some research on how to get a literary agent. She sent queries to literary agents. "With the first manuscript, I sent out hundreds of emails that included the first three chapters and a summary of the book. By the third manuscript, I'd learned how to query smarter." Agents get hundreds of queries a day, so Jamie knows it's difficult to get noticed without major credentials or a publishing history. "It's very hard for me to take a compliment, but I felt that I had some credibility when I finally got an agent and she actually sold two of my books."

Her debut novel, entitled *In the Cards*, which released in 2014, deals with fate, self-discovery, and love. One early reader told Jamie that reading her novel allowed her to crystallize something personal. "That was incredible, to know that I helped someone with one of my stories."

So does a romance novel have explicit sex scenes, and what would her 13-year-old daughter think? Jamie says that her novels deal more with the emotional side of relationships, but, "Yes, they include explicit sex scenes. Most romance novels do these days." She hopes her daughter won't read them until she's much older. Her husband reads her work too and says, "Wait a minute, I don't see myself in your hero." Jamie laughs, replying, "It's fiction, honey."

Jamie has created her own romance novelist persona through her blog and social media and says, "I never thought I could do this." She is now a regular at national conventions and when others ask her advice she says,

"The most important step of the whole process was to just sit down and do it. My hobby has become a second career. Who knew?"

TAKEAWAY

- Jamie loved writing, and she loved the idea of writing a novel so much that she just jumped in and did it.
- Research and writing groups helped her learn how to structure her work.

IZUP: Darcy Ahl

Another example showing the benefits of research comes from Darcy Ahl. She launched a phone application that stops teens from using their phone when the phone is traveling at more than five miles an hour. This app prevents teens from talking or texting while driving. Figuring out how to create an application, particularly one that is so involved, required a great deal of research.

"In my wildest dreams I never thought I'd be a software entrepreneur," this venture mom declared. So how did Darcy Ahl go from riding with her 16-year old son on Interstate 95 to running a start-up? It all started with an experience she had when her son had his learner's permit. He was driving and Darcy was a passenger when both of their phones rang. Darcy answered hers to speak with a client and her son didn't hesitate before fumbling in his pocket to retrieve his phone. His driving immediately became erratic and dangerous, causing Darcy to hang up and ask her son to do the same.

Upon returning to her office, Darcy sat down across from her partner at the executive recruiting firm where she worked and commented that she wasn't ready to be the mother of a teenage driver. She said, "I wish there was something that would stop kids from using their phones while driving." And they realized that this was an important idea that they could run with. Initially thinking along the lines of a chip in the phone, Darcy and her partner began their research. They happened to be recruiters for engineers so they made a few phone calls that day to friends in the field and found out that a GPS system could be used. A few more phone calls the next day and they found the right people to build the app.

So in just a couple of days they found out what they would need to move forward. But unlike so many small ventures, their venture needed funding to hire a team of software engineers. The plan was to develop a GPS-based phone application that would turn a phone off when it was traveling at more than five miles an hour.

"Sending your child out the door with a set of keys is frightening enough without the thought of them being distracted by talking or texting on the phone. Phones are a lifeline to teens, they can't help themselves; they feel they must answer." Darcy learned through online research that 7,000 teens die every year in auto accidents. "If our application could shut out those distractions—no texting, no talking, no checking Facebook, no tweeting—we knew we would have something valuable."

With funding from friends, family, and angel investors, a start-up team was assembled in Massachusetts, a hotbed of technology talent. After a successful beta test of the application, IZUP (pronounced Eyes Up) was born. Some people ask about what happens if you have the application and you are a passenger in a car and your phone turns off. In response, Darcy suggests a novel idea, "Why not have a real conversation as a family on the way to Grandma's house for Thanksgiving?" IZUP does offer a password-protected override.

Illume Software, the developer of IZUP, is working with insurance companies to offer discounts for drivers who use the application. Expansion plans include international markets and additional uses for their location-based technology. With a nine-member team running the company, Darcy is free to focus on getting the word out about IZUP. As the Vice President of Public Affairs, she spends her time hosting events around the country for teens, parents, and others. While still working as an executive recruiter, Darcy splits her time between the two companies. Her children, ages 20, 18, and 13, often attend presentations and serve on the teen advisory board of the company.

From the idea to her first sale took three and a half years. Darcy said, "There have been many ups and down and mistakes along the way. You have to have a lot of grit and desire to bring your idea to life. Sometimes you feel like you're at the edge of a cliff, but if one life is saved by our application, it will all be worth it."

TAKEAWAY

- Things were set in motion in one afternoon with just a few phone calls.
- Although this venture was a long-term project that involved funding and building a team, Darcy was able to determine through her research what was involved in a matter of weeks.

If you're considering a tech-based venture, you're probably aware that creating an app has become easier and less expensive than it was in the past. Many creators use overseas developers who are well versed in delivering a finished product in a timely manner (often in just a few weeks) for a reasonable price (under $5,000).

If you realize that your venture will require long-term research or requires waiting for some type of certification or classes, work this week toward building a timeline for completing any necessary items. This may delay your progress—and that's okay as long as you set a date to move forward.

You may also want to revisit your idea. It's okay to realize that you've chosen something that is simply not feasible, would require too much outside assistance, or would require large amounts of funding. Entrepreneurs need to be able to assess and pivot if necessary.

Now that you've chosen your venture, let's give it a name. We'll do that in Week 4.

II

GET
ORGANIZED

four

Week 4:
Name Your Venture

To welcome Kyle's family to her neighborhood, Heather delivered a batch of her Grandma Ida's Jumble cookies. Kyle had never tasted anything like them. After they became fast friends, she said to Heather, "We should sell your cookies." Since their kids devoured this healthy, high-fiber snack, Heather and Kyle thought it would be fun to offer the cookies at a school fund-raiser to see if there was a market for the product. The cookies were a hit and they were in business. To name their venture, the two women wanted something that evoked sharing—sharing between Grandma Ida and her granddaughter, between a mom and child, or between two friends—so they came up with the perfect name, "You & Me Cookie."

Naming your venture is one of the most exciting aspects of getting started, but it can also be one of the most difficult to do. It's an important step to spend time on. A great name can propel your venture forward and a bad name can actually stall it. So how do you come up with a great name?

WEEK 4 ASSIGNMENTS

During this week, use the six-step process outlined in this chapter to come up with a great name for your venture.

Assignment #1: Brainstorm Related Words

In this assignment, you'll come up with as many words as possible to identify your product or service. You'll start by writing down what you are offering and then below it write down as many related ideas, synonyms, opposites, puns, etc. as you can think of. For example, if you are starting a dessert business, you might list sugar, cupcakes, pies, Bundt cakes, cookies, brownies, lemon bars . . . anything related to desserts. When you can't think of any more words, search online using a synonym finder, such as Visual Thesaurus (www.visualthesaurus.com), to add more words to your list. Then, add adjectives. For a dessert business, you might add words like yummy, delicious, tasty, sweet, luscious, delectable, scrumptious, and so on.

While brainstorming, jot down the keywords that could link to your website. Think like a potential customer; what words would they type into a search engine to find a product or service like yours? For example, if your product is nontoxic skin care, a shopper might include some of the following words in her search: beauty, organic, skin care, healthy, all natural, and toxin-free. Keywords help you to expand the list of words you can use to develop your name.

 IN YOUR NOTEBOOK

Create three lists to describe your product or service.

> List #1: Your product or service and as many related ideas, synonyms, opposites, puns, etc. as you can.
> List #2: Record every adjective you can think of that describes your product or service.
> List #3: Record any word a customer might type into a search engine to find a product or service similar to yours.

Assignment #2: Get Personal

Now, let's focus on the strictly personal. Names of people, places, or things that mean something to you may also be a perfect choice for your venture's name. These could be things like your name, your kids' names, your pet's name, a favorite vacation spot, your street name, your school's name, or your home state. Think of a family name, a grandparent's middle name, a cousin's nickname, or your nickname. Consider your state flower or state animal, your astrological sign, or your hometown team's mascot. The ideas are endless. What else is related to your venture? For example, if you are from the Carolinas and starting a line of girl's clothing, your venture name could be "Carolina Girls," which is a play on a song, or "Sweet Caroline" or "Tar Heel Togs"—you get the idea. For a dessert business, the name could be "Tar Heel Treats" or "Carolina Confections."

 IN YOUR NOTEBOOK

List #4: Write down the names of things, persons, or places that are meaningful to you.

Assignment #3: Incorporate the Purpose of Your Venture

Now write down the purpose of your venture. (Think back to the work you did in Chapter 2, when you explored the directions your venture might take.) Include words for all the possible ways you can see your product or service being used. Using the dessert business example, your purpose could be to provide desserts for parties and special occasions. Now you'll create another list of words: party, celebration, fete, and gala. Go to the synonym finder again and add words related to this list. By now you should have several long lists that will give you lots of ideas to choose from. How about "Southern Gala Girls," "Your Go-To Gala Girl," or "Carolina Celebrations"?

 IN YOUR NOTEBOOK

List #5: Write down all the words you can think of that could describe the purpose of your product or service.

Assignment #4: Create Catchy Combinations and Add a Tag Line

You want a name that people will remember, something that describes who you are and what you do. When I was looking for a name for my venture, I thought about what I love doing and what I am. I love launching new ventures and I'm a mom. So VentureMom became the embodiment of all that I do and the name tells my story.

Now you are ready to start combining words from your lists to create catchy, memorable combinations. Think about common sayings or clichés. Look at words that start with the same letter, as in "Southern Gala Girls" or "Southern Sweets"—alliteration can be a powerful tool in naming a venture. Rhyming words can also work.

Your name should clearly tell what you do. If your name doesn't tell exactly what you do, add a tag line. Some examples are "Fabulous Fetes: Party Planning for You" or "Gorgeous Galas: Everything for Your Event" or "Susie's Sweets: Delicious Desserts for Every Occasion." You get the idea. The tag line should be a statement telling what you do in just a few words. It should appear everywhere after your venture's name. (You'll find more information on choosing a tag line in Chapter 5.)

 IN YOUR NOTEBOOK

- Using the lists you compiled in the first three assignments, make a list of possible combinations for the name of your venture. Write down as many combinations as you can.
- If your venture name requires a tag line, make a list of the possibilities. The tag line should be a short phrase that tells what you do.

Assignment #5: Gather Feedback

Once you come up with some names you like, get feedback from family, friends, and potential customers. Use these names in sentences or practice telling these names to a potential client. For example, imagine you are talking with an old friend and you say, "I've started a new venture doing _____ (briefly describe what you do); it's called _____ (fill in your name)." Does it roll off your tongue and make sense? Is it easy to say and spell—and, most important, to remember?

 IN YOUR NOTEBOOK

Make a list of possible names for your venture. Share these with friends, family, and potential customers and record their feedback.

Assignment #6: Check Domain Availability

From the time you start to put your venture out there to potential clients, your name will be linked to everything you do. All advertising will center on your brand. Spend the time to get this right. Check the Internet for similar names and see if the domain name (website address, or URL) is available (www.instantdomainsearch.com). If so, once you decide on a name, claim the domain right away. It may be gone the next time you look. You can do this through a hosting package for about $10 a year. You don't want to spend time and effort creating a name and then find out it's already taken when you start creating your website. (Chapter 7 shows you how to get started on the Web.) If "yourcompanyname.com" is taken by the time you start your web page, you may need to go back to square one.

Taking this one step further, you can protect your brand and name for around $325 by registering a trademark through the U.S. government trademark office (www.uspto.gov). This is valuable to do if you have plans to go beyond the local area with your venture. If you apply for a trademark for your venture name, make a note of any pertinent information (date of application, contacts, etc.) in your Notebook.

Quick Tips for Naming Your Venture
Choose a name that:
Is clever, creative, and memorable.
Is easy to pronounce and spell.
Clearly tells what you do.
Represents all that you do.
Avoids negative words.
Includes keywords customers might use when searching online.
Has an available domain name.

Venture Names to Love
Here are some of my all-time favorites:

* Vintage Vogue: vintage jewelry.
* Leftover Luxuries: roving tag sales with leftover items from designers and clients.
* Birdy and Grace: golf wear for women (Grace is the founder's daughter's name).

- Smart Playrooms: a service that reorganizes your playroom.
- Greening Our Children: a charity to educate parents on how to be more green.
- Easel Does It: an art class for young children.
- The Common Courtesy: a manners class for kids.
- Secrets of a Home Cook: a cooking blog.
- Soggy Doggy Doormat: doormats for dogs.
- Gum Drop Swap: a consignment website for children's clothes.
- The Cooking Fairy: nightly meals for families.
- Order Out of Chaos: an organizer for kids with ADD.

By now your creative juices should be flowing with ideas for naming your venture. Choosing your venture's name is a very important decision. Dedicate the time this week to following the six-step process outlined in this chapter. Having a meaningful, relevant, and catchy name will resonate with your potential customers and will help you brand your company effectively.

You'll need to come up with a name this week—even if it's not perfect. Moving forward will help you to launch your business within 12 weeks.

NAMING YOUR VENTURE SUCCESS STORIES

In the success stories that follow, you'll see how several moms came up with creative, catchy names for their businesses.

8 to the Bar: Kathy Monahan

When Kathy Monahan created a natural nut and fruit bar with her business partner, Jim, she wanted a name centered around his love of music. There are eight notes in a musical bar and eight ingredients in their product. "8 to the Bar" was catchy and told a story that reflected both the product and its founders.

Kathy Monahan's move to New Hampshire with her family allowed her to explore all kinds of healthy outdoor activities. Spending long hours outdoors hiking and skiing with her kids, Kathy felt she was getting back to nature. Eating natural food went hand in hand with this new life, and eating healthy snack bars became a part of her regular routine.

At a family gathering back in Connecticut, Kathy's cousin's husband, Jim Bruno, served a delicious nut, oat, and fruit bar made from a recipe that he had developed on his own. Kathy loved it. Thinking of her own search for great snack bars, she and Jim put their heads together and decided to go into the bar-making business. She said, "As an exercise enthusiast, I was always looking for a healthy, delicious bar, and I knew there was a need for something like the bar Jim made."

So they began to get organized. First, they needed a name. Since Jim is a musician, he wanted to use a musical theme. The bar that Jim created had a total of eight nuts, oats, and fruits, so they came up with "8 to the Bar." Kathy's cousin Donna (Jim's wife), a graphic designer, took the name and created a logo and label with a musical note on it. The name and the image capture the product and the venture perfectly.

The two sourced ingredients and found a commercial kitchen that they could rent on an hourly basis to create their bars. Kathy says, "We got a lot of advice. Lloyd of The Double L Market in Westport, Connecticut, was a great source of information and our first customer." When their first batch was ready, Lloyd said, "Bring in twelve bars. If they sell, you're in the store." Two days later, Lloyd called for more. At this point, they spent time perfecting the recipe for larger batches. They also decided to offer a box of bites. After Kathy and Jim visited other local stores, markets, and exercise studios with samples, the orders began to come in.

Kathy spends 20 hours a week or more in the kitchen and more hours delivering boxes of the bars. "We do everything ourselves, from making the bars, to packaging, to delivery. My kids are older so this business couldn't have come at a better time because I have more time."

Kathy is happy to point out that the venture is profitable, and she also says it's great to have a business partner. "We each have a different skill set and a huge level of respect for each other; it's a very positive relationship." On the future of 8 to the Bar, she says, "We want to be in Whole Foods and all over the country."

TAKEAWAY

- Look at your interests and talents when deciding on a name.
- Think about how a logo could work with your name. The musical note and play on words for 8 to the Bar is catchy and memorable.

Tuckadream Pillows: Sarina Galu

When her son couldn't sleep, Sarina Galu found a solution that grew into a venture. A seamstress, Sarina named her venture "Tuckadream Pillows" after the pillow with a pocket for dreams she created for her little boy. This is one of my favorite naming stories.

Nightmares can be scary at all ages, but when Sarina Galu's three-year-old son Tucker woke up from bad dreams for the fourth night in a row, she needed a solution. Her son was looking for security. His blankie had long since disintegrated and was reduced to a few scraps of fabric kept in a Ziploc bag. After doing some research on what might help Tucker sleep through the night, Sarina decided to sew him a special sleep pillow and then took it one step further.

She fashioned the pillow with a small pocket to hold a nighttime dream journal. After talking with Tucker about what he wanted to dream about instead of the scary things that kept waking him up, Sarina wrote his happy thoughts in a small notebook. They called this his "dreamkeeper journal," and Sarina and Tucker used it to substitute good dreams and wishes for scary thoughts and nightmares. With his happy thoughts tucked into the pillow, Sarina tucked Tucker in with the motto, "Positive thoughts, positive dreams."

Suddenly, sweet dreams replaced Tucker's nightmares, and he woke up refreshed and energetic. While Tucker's experience may be unique, he found reassurance by sleeping with the pillow, knowing that his happy thoughts were safely written down.

The pillow has other uses too. The pocket on the pillow became a place not only for Tucker's dreamkeeper journal but also for things like birthday lists, prayers, and letters to Santa and the Tooth Fairy.

The name "Tuckadream" incorporated both personal and functional aspects of Sarina's product: her son's name, the act of tucking him into bed each night, and the pocket for his dream journal. Sarina created pillows for friends and family and the response was overwhelming. Sarina was chatting about her venture when she learned that her neighbor's husband happened to be in the business of fabricating soft goods, including pillows. Sarina was able to use his manufacturing facilities to create a small run of pillows so she could test the viability of her idea. She self-funded the first run. The business went from an idea in April to producing 100 pillows on her first production run in August.

Sarina created her own website and began to market the Tuckadream Pillow through emails to friends and at small fairs in the area. The Children's Hospital in New York ordered 20 pillows to use in helping their patients journal about positive dreams for healthy outcomes. This segment of her business has great potential. "It makes me happy to see that my idea, conceived to help my son, is also helping others," says Sarina. "It's also a great way to teach children the virtues of goal setting."

"It was my family and friends who motivated me to share my creation to help other kids who were facing the same issues that Tucker had been dealing with. I never thought it would turn into a business." Sarina now sells the product in specialty toy stores, hospitals, hotel gift shops, at local fairs, and through the Tuckadream website.

With two boys ages six and four, Sarina says, "The pillow helps our family end the day on a positive note and I hope it will help other families to have thoughtful bedtime discussions about what their children want to dream about, wish for, or be when they grow up. Perhaps we as parents should end our days by writing in our own journals—we might sleep better too."

TAKEAWAY

- Sarina had a word with several meanings from which to build a name: Tucker, her son's name; getting tucked into bed; and tucking desired dreams in the pillow. Not everyone will be so lucky to have a name with multiple associations with their venture—but use your creativity and you'll come up with something that works.
- Consider words that have meaning to you and that apply to your product or service.

Sam-I-Am Media: Samantha Loomis

When Samantha Loomis started a business around developing photo books for others, she had no idea what to name her venture. Her husband suggested a play on her name. "All I kept thinking of was the Dr. Seuss books and the quote 'Sam I am,' so I named my venture "Sam-I-Am Media." It's a great name that people remember.

How many of us have boxes of old photos waiting to be put into albums? Or files of photos on our computers? Or stacks of videotapes that should be on DVDs before they deteriorate? Many people look at those piles and shove everything back in the closet. Samantha Loomis saw a venture in this situation.

From her previous job in the magazine industry, Sam had some experience arranging photos to tell a story. She was an avid photographer, and one year she organized the family's summer photos into a book for her parents. She used online photo sites to create their summer story, and she gave them the album as a gift. They loved it. And then her parents asked Sam to make albums for their friends.

Realizing she had a talent others could use, she offered to prepare photo albums as a business venture. Her first sales were to friends and family, and then word of mouth expanded her client base. She was asked to put together albums highlighting special birthdays, anniversaries, and graduations, or albums of special trips. "Mother's and Father's Day albums are a big request," Sam says. "Grandparents love getting a photo book of their grandchildren that they can carry around. Another hit is 'A Year in the Life' family books. These document the life of a family each year."

Using sites like Snapfish and Shutterfly, Sam can cull from photo files downloaded by different family members to create a single album. The client provides captions and approves Sam's choices of photos and layouts. Sam is happy to give instruction in uploading photos to anyone who might be unfamiliar with the sites. She can also scan in a lifetime of paper photos so that box of old pictures becomes digitized, preserving them and making them easier to work with. She does conversion of videos into DVDs so that those memories can be shared via computer.

Sam has two children and is able to do most of her work during the day while they're in school. Sam thrives on organization and enjoys her work, putting to good use her talent for seeing a timeline through photos. She currently works between 10 and 20 hours a week and charges for her time.

Sam built on her existing skills and taught herself the finer points of the photo sites her customers use. This made it easy for her to put together interesting books with multiple options in terms of photo sizes, layouts, and album covers. "So many people don't have the time to create a memory book or DVD that they want to share." Sam can make this happen.

TAKEAWAY

- Don't overthink it. Sometimes the first choice is the best choice.
- Choose something catchy and then add a tag line to explain the venture.

———

Get busy nailing down and registering a name this week, because *next* week is all about branding. Branding can make or break your venture. You'll come up with a logo, colors, and a tag line. All of these elements will work to define your venture and your brand.

five

Week 5:
Develop Your Brand
(This Is the Fun Part)

When her dog tracked snow and mud all over her house one winter, Joanne needed a solution. She noticed the shag carpet–like material used at the carwash and thought that would make a perfect mat to soak up all the muck her dog brought in. After finding the manufacturer in China, she created her product and placed her first order. Her venture's name tells you what the product is and her logo shows you exactly what it does. The colors she chose—light blue on a navy background—do a great job of reinforcing the watery theme. When you see her logo, you know it's her and the Soggy Doggy Doormat.

When you see the swoosh, you think of Nike. When you see the yellow arches, you think of McDonald's. When you hear, "Leave off the last S for savings," you know it's Sleepy's. You want your clients to think of you when they see your logo, colors, and tag line. This week you'll put together the elements that make up your venture's brand. Remember, it doesn't have to be perfect, or a permanent choice, but you'll need to decide on something this week in order to launch your venture within 12 weeks.

WEEK 5 ASSIGNMENTS

Branding can be fun. Get creative and get some input. Many of the moms I've interviewed told me that their kids actually helped them come up with not only their names but also the venture's colors and logo. This is where the rubber meets the road, so if you need creative help, make sure to get it. You have a lot to do this week. Work to complete all your assignments so you can move forward.

Assignment #1: Design Your Logo

Branding identifies your venture and differentiates your business from competing or similar ventures. The branding process begins with designing your logo. It doesn't have to be professionally done; you can design something using various fonts and clip art. But your logo should represent who you are and what you offer. When I was designing the VentureMom logo, I wanted to use the initials in the name because of how nicely the letters fit together. I liked the V next to the M with the Web address below it surrounded by the rectangle. Very simple, but when you see it, you know it's me.

Experiment with different fonts and styles to see what fits with your venture. Look at the logos other name brands have chosen. For example, the red script of Coca-Cola is so immediately recognizable you know what it is without really seeing the letters. There are many sites on the Web that can help you create a logo: logomaker.com, 99designs.com, and flamingtext.com are just a few; see the Resources section at the end of the book for others. Many of these are free or charge a nominal amount.

You can also find a friend or colleague (present or past) who is talented in graphic design to help you. Think of what you can barter with her. If you make a great carrot cake, offer one for her help. Or if your venture is to teach Pilates classes, offer her a free class. If you don't know anyone, send an email to family and friends to ask for a referral.

Fonts have personalities, and you want one that speaks to what you do. For example, the logo for a children's product could incorporate a fun font like MV Boli (*MV Boli*), whereas a logo for a computer business might require a more serious font like Arial Black (**Arial Black**). Many fonts are readily available with most software products. You can also buy fonts. What is important is that you not let this decision delay you from designing your logo this week. Choose something and move on. Use the same font or a companion font in everything that's connected with your business. This means that for everything that the public sees, the font(s) you choose should convey an image that's consistent with your brand.

Browse through what other companies have done to get ideas for your logo and font. Put ideas and sketches of things you like in your Notebook. Choose something that speaks to you. Create a few samples and get feedback from family and friends, but remember it's yours to like and live with.

Keep all your notes and ideas in your Notebook.

Assignment #2: Choose Your Colors

For the VentureMom logo, I wanted two colors that represented what my message was all about. Brown conveyed strength with style for the business side and pink represented moms, so I used Brown for the V (Venture) and pink for the M (Mom). Look at common colors that many businesses use. Red and yellow are food colors, which is why fast-food outlets use them. Think McDonald's, Burger King, and Wendy's—they all use red and yellow. Multiple studies have been done on what various colors represent to consumers. Blue is typically a business color (think IBM).

Studies have shown that too many colors can be confusing to potential clients; fewer colors are easier to remember. Most large brands use one main color and highlight with a second color. WalMart and JetBlue both use a cheery blue and highlight their sales and action steps with orange. Color contrast is important. Best Buy uses navy blue and highlights with a bright yellow. Nike contrasts black with orange.

Be consistent. UPS is known for brown, but their website is mostly teal, their accent color. Color consistency creates a sense of familiarity for customers and users. It gives clients a level of comfort and trust when they buy from you or use your service. Your colors will appear on everything you do, and they should be the same shade in every application.

Choose two colors that speak to you and your product—who you are, what you are offering, and what makes you feel happy and energized. Get a paint wheel from a hardware or paint store and play with various combinations. Go online, print out the colors, and put them in your Notebook. Sleep on your choices and look again. What do you feel when you look at your color choices? You want to feel good about your colors. Remember it doesn't have to be perfect. Choose your colors this week.

Assignment #3: Add a Tag Line

Many names require a tag line that explains or clarifies the purpose of the venture. And even if your name doesn't require one, a tag line helps define your brand by giving you a line that you can use in different places, such as your website, your packaging, and your business cards. A tag line is the phrase that helps people link your name to your brand message. It's a marketing statement meant to serve as a customer magnet. Here are a few examples of well-known tag lines that are descriptive and helpful:

"Just do it" (Nike)
"What's in Your Wallet?" (Capital One)
"Think outside the bun" (Taco Bell)
"Eat Fresh" (Subway)
"When you care enough to send the very best" (Hallmark)
"The nighttime sniffling sneezing coughing aching stuffy head fever so
      you can rest medicine" (Nyquil)

Some of these are funny, some are descriptive, but all of them make you think. You want to develop a tag line like one of these that will make people think and remember your venture.

If your name does not communicate what your business does, or if your business is new, use a descriptive tag line to bridge the gap. A well-known business, or one whose name communicates what the business is, can use an expressive tag line to further communicate the essence and personality of the brand.

What do you want your tag line to say about your service or product? Think of it as an opportunity to expand on your name and logo to tell clients what you're all about. The founders of You & Me Cookie use "for the cookie connoisseur" as their tag line, and it can be found on all of their marketing and packaging.

For my own businesses, VentureMom.com, the tag line is "Products & Services, By & For Moms. " This tells users what my site is all about. Another mom who created a sports stick holder called StickStorage uses the tag line, "Your Gear Goes Here." (You'll read about her later in this chapter.)

Look at what other businesses are using for ideas as you create a tag line that works for you. And again, go to the Web, where you'll find some great resources that offer assistance like taglineguru.com, sloganmania.com, and slogan4u.com. Be sure to make it understandable and not too clever; you don't want users to have to decipher what it means. Here are more great examples to get your creative ideas flowing.

Familiar Tag Lines

Businesses

Target
    Expect More, Pay Less

Allstate
    You're in good hands with Allstate

Food

Burger King
    Have it your way.

Lucky Charms
    Magically delicious.

DiGiorno
    It's not delivery. It's DiGiorno.

M&Ms
    Melts in your mouth, not in your hands.

Consumer Products

Bounty
    The quicker picker-upper.

Gillette Dry Idea
    Never let 'em see you sweat.

Charmin
    Please don't squeeze the Charmin.

L'Oréal
    Because I'm worth it.

 IN YOUR NOTEBOOK

- Record examples of tag lines used by businesses offering products or services similar to yours.
- Make a list of possible tag lines for your venture.

Assignment #4: Create Business Cards

Even though business cards may soon be a thing of the past, it's still a good idea to have them. While many people use cell phones to exchange contact information, a business card makes a statement. It says, "I'm in business, and here's how you can reach me. " In addition to an email address, a potential client has a tangible reminder of you and your venture.

When you meet someone and tell them what you do, you'll want to be able to hand them a card so they can reach you. Use your logo and tag line together with your contact info.

Your business card should include the following information in your chosen colors and font:

- Name
- Business name
- Logo

- Email address
- Website
- Phone number(s)

For some of you, a physical address and a snail-mail address are necessary, for others, they can be dispensed with. If you are only dealing with customers and clients through email, then leave this information off. If you need to be physically accessible (customer pickup, for example), include it. Consider repeating your name along with your venture's name and tag line on the back of the card, and perhaps a very brief description of what you do.

Sites like vistaprint.com and Moo.com make it very easy and inexpensive to download your artwork and get your cards quickly. There are many different sizes and paper stocks to choose from. Look at other cards that you like and create something that speaks to you. These sites can help you. Don't let wanting your business cards to be perfect stop you. You'll need them when you start telling everyone you know about your new venture.

 ## IN YOUR NOTEBOOK

Record the information you plan to include on your business card, including notes about your logo and the font and colors you plan to use.

It's important to brand yourself and your venture so that, like McDonald's golden arches, when people see your logo, colors, and tag line, they'll know it's you.

BRANDING SUCCESS STORIES

In the stories below you'll see how these moms created memorable brands. Get your inspiration from these venture paths to build your own brand.

Not all brands need a tag line, as Tara Michelle, our first example below, shows. Their mermaid logo *is* their brand.

Tara Michelle: Tara Vessels and Michelle Mauboussin

When Tara Vessels and Michelle Mauboussin were looking for a name for their line of beach coverups, they decided on Tara Michelle. Not only did it use both their names, but the feedback they received was overwhelmingly positive. The name was easy to say and remember. But they knew they needed colors and an image to convey the essence of their company. Since their products are designed to be used on a hot day at the beach, they chose orange for the sun and aqua for the ocean. And what symbolizes fun times at the beach more than a mermaid? By choosing a font in all lowercase and a turquoise background with a coral mermaid, they put together the elements of a brand that is easy to recognize and tells their story.

Who knew they could launch a business while running together? Tara Vessels and Michelle Mauboussin both worked in fashion in New York City, but kids pulled them out of their careers for a while. They had always said that when they got their first child off to college they would lay the groundwork for a venture that would be their focus as their kids grew up and left home.

Tara and Michelle's running group meets three to four times a week for a 5- to 10-mile run. Logging all these miles together gave them lots of time to talk. All that talk turned into planning a business. Two factors led them to create Tara Michelle: the desire to focus on a product that brings to mind fun and relaxation, and the fact that they weren't able to find a beach coverup that looked great, was priced well, and above all, fit well.

Their own needs, as well as their love of the beach, inspired their line of coverups and sarongs. Michelle said, "When I worked for Elie Tahari, his main focus was on fit, so that was instilled in me as a top priority for our coverups." Tara added, "We wanted something that was flattering and could be worn from the beach to the street." Once they had settled on their product, they turned their attention to choosing a company name and logo. The name they settled on, Tara Michelle, got great feedback from a fellow entrepreneur, and Tara Michelle was born.

Then the research on production began in earnest with the two moms self-funding their venture. They drew on their contacts and their previous experience in the fashion industry to find patternmakers, to source fabrics and trims, and to find a manufacturer for their designs. Through a process of trial and error they finally found their sources and perfected their fit. Tara said, "It wasn't so glamorous; at one point we were trying on coverups in a McDonald's bathroom on 7th Avenue," but they both laugh, saying they will always remember how it all started. While this part of the process took longer than a week to complete, they were moving forward with the product design every day. While they were waiting, they worked on their website and marketing ideas.

Finally they had their samples. Tara's daughter had worked for a boutique that had six stores in resort communities in the Northeast. Tara sent a photo of her daughter wearing the Tara Michelle tunic and suggested a meeting. Driving to Boston for their first sample showing, the two women were not sure what to expect, but that boutique gave them a large order for all six stores. This was their first sale, and they were already in the black and on their way.

They hit the road to show the line to other boutiques and do trunk shows, and they are working to build brand recognition and manage their growth. At every trunk show—an event where someone opens her home to several vendors who showcase their wares to her local circle of friends—Tara Michelle's logo and colors are prominently featured in a large sign and in their table decor. The label for their clothing matches their logo, extending their branding. They had been in business for less than a year when they took a big leap by opting for a Tara Michelle booth at the Moda show held at the Javits Center in New York City, where their logo attracted attention, and their coverups drew interest from new and old customers alike. Their investment (a booth at the Moda show doesn't come cheap) paid off. Their strong brand ID helped them garner orders from resorts and boutiques around the country.

Their distribution center began in Michelle's house. "We wanted to watch our finances and only spend what we brought in at the start."

With eight kids between them, it's been a family affair. The kids have helped with website design, production, modeling, photography, and tech support. "We love that our kids are involved; they've been a huge help." And their logo, with its playful image and happy colors, is found on all that they do. Just as the large T did for Tori Burch, the Tara Michelle logo is helping to establish this new brand.

Both women say, "This is not a hobby. This is a full-time venture but since we're both mothers, we understand that family comes first." So how has their venture been getting validation so soon. "We felt strongly about our product vision and the early success has inspired us to work harder. "

TAKEAWAY

- Sometimes your own name can make a great name for your business.
- Seek feedback from other entrepreneurs.
- Choose colors that speak to your product and brand.

Stick Storage: Kim Genzburg

Another great example of using branding to tell your story comes from Kim Genzburg of Stick Storage. Not only does the name tell you that her product stores sticks—lacrosse, hockey, mop, and broom sticks—but her logo also shows you how. And her tag line says it all: "Your Gear Goes Here." You need only see the logo to know it's the Stick Storage brand.

When she renovated her home, she finally had a proper mudroom, but lacrosse, field hockey, and ice hockey sticks magically multiplied and still ended up on the floor. Kim Genzburg needed a solution, so she built one. Taking a small wooden table, she drilled holes in the top and painted it. "It was a skinny table that fit behind the door. The kids could drop their sticks in and get to them easily."

When friends came over and saw this cool solution, they wanted their own. Kim realized she had come up with something that didn't exist and began to research the possibility of making her product and selling it. "I really knew nothing about manufacturing but I did have background in furniture sales. I talked to everyone I knew, and people were so nice and so helpful."

Realizing she would need a plastic that wouldn't crack, fade, warp, or stain, Kim spent time finding the right plastics company that could build a prototype of what she envisioned. "I wanted pieces that would easily snap together to support the "grab and go" design idea and I wanted multiple primary colors to match interiors or team colors." Once Kim had the product concept nailed down, she was ready to find a name. "Stick Storage" was short and it told a story. Done.

Kim wanted her Stick Storage unit to be made in America, not only to support U.S. manufacturing but also to allow her to be able to touch and feel the product and know what needed to be tweaked. "I found a small company that I could work with in New York State. The owner was able to deliver my Stick Storage in seven colors but I would have to order 50 in each color, and this was scary."

Kim says she almost shelved the idea, thinking, "Can I really do this by myself? Will it sell? Can I build a company on a single idea?" But she loves to challenge herself and says, "Creating a successful business out of thin air is definitely a challenge."

Kim and her husband asked all of their friends what they thought of the idea and got only positive feedback. Friends with backgrounds in business management gave Kim a great, speedy education in business development. Armed with this information, she felt comfortable using savings to fund her venture. She also found a mentor at the national, federally funded group called Score (Service Corps of Retired Executives), which supports start-ups and small businesses. Kim was paired with a mentor who had a background in plastics, and he helped guide her with product development.

Now she had a product, but she needed to complete her branding. Coming up with the name Stick Storage gave her a strong start because it tells what the product does. The logo was instrumental as well by showing how the product works. When you see her logo, you know what her product is. And her tag line seals the deal: Your Gear Goes Here.

She had been selling to friends and family but the real test came as Kim took her product out to area lacrosse tournaments (direct selling is a key part of her sales plan). Kim has networked with other moms to have them work as sales reps in other parts of the country. "This was easy. I knew friends who were sitting on lacrosse fields in other places and asked them to set up a sales table. It's the perfect job for a mom who has to attend a three-day tournament anyway."

Kim teamed up with a large lacrosse retailer that serves as her warehouse and distribution center. How did she do this? She took her Stick Storage unit to the store and asked to speak to the owner. After a short conversation, the two struck a deal. The store would carry the product and

Kim could store her inventory there. She is lucky to have solved this piece of the puzzle. With a trademark in hand and a patent pending, Kim is on her way to having the whole venture puzzle solved.

TAKEAWAY

- Kim's logo shows exactly what the product does. Create one for your venture that does the same.
- Choose colors that embody what you offer. Or just colors you like. Again, don't overthink it, but remember your colors will be part of your brand and on everything you do.
- Develop a tag line that tells what your product does or your service provides.

Vicolo Mio: Doreen Godfrey

Creating a brand for fashion accessories came easily to Doreen Godfrey. Italy was a part of her life, so it became a part of her venture. Following her own path in life translated to her tag line, "Follow Your Own Trend," which captures the spirit of her accessories venture. Doreen kept it simple with teal and black and used different fonts, but her logo, like her brand, is stylish and distinctive.

Italy, where she has family, and fashion, which is her passion, have been big influences in her life, and the two came together to epitomize her venture. While traveling in Verona one day, Doreen Godfrey came across a street sign that read *Vicolo,* or in English, "pathway." Having always dreamt of starting her own business, she was struck by a thought—*Vicolo Mio!* My Path.

She had a career that took her from the receptionist desk at *Seventeen* magazine to national sales at BCBG. But, as she points out, "When I left fashion to become a mother, I had to recreate my wardrobe for my new life with children."

To indulge her love of fashion, Doreen turned to accessories to create a look that suited her new life. "I would throw on a scarf, bracelet, and earrings to pull a look together. Women started asking me where I got all of my accessories. I thought there might be a business idea in those requests." Doreen decided to reach out to her fashion contacts to explore the process of buying accessories wholesale. She found a source and funded her first batch of inventory from her savings. Her new venture would be an accessories boutique in her home.

The branding of Vicolo Mio, which got its start that day in Verona, was based on the idea of how Italian women add a scarf or necklace and look fashionably pulled together. Her name and her tag line—"Follow Your Own Trend"—underscore that idea. Her branding is a bit more subtle than that of some other ventures, but Vicolo Mio's stylish presentation conveys her brand message perfectly.

She got to work gathering a line of accessories from vendors in New York City. Her kids' playroom became her shop. Vicolo Mio carries necklaces, bracelets, rings, scarves, handbags, and seasonal accessories— all the fun things needed to turn jeans and a T-shirt into an outfit. "Women always want to look stylish, and in the current economy, accessories are an inexpensive and easy way to change a base outfit."

She launched her venture with a three-day event in her home and used her personal email list of locals to spread the word. Shoppers at the event started sending photos of pieces they loved to friends on their phones and telling them to come to the sale. The Vicolo Mio event went viral, just like a high school party.

With a three-year-old and a one-year-old, Doreen isn't ready for a storefront just yet. She's happy with scheduled sales and the "by appointment" boutique in her home.

"I love that I can get my fashion fix and share my love of accessories with women who are looking to spruce up their look without spending a lot." Her advice on fashion? "Follow your own trend."

TAKEAWAY

- Doreen chose a name, two fonts, and colors that she feels embody the style she is offering. Sometimes simple is best.
- A great tag line can intrigue and inspire. Make sure your tag line does this for your venture.

―――――

With your logo, colors, and tag line established, you're ready to price your product or service. Soldier on to Week 6.

six

Week 6:
Price Your Product

She took large-scale photos of nature for enjoyment and to display in her own home. But when the local library asked Lynne Byrne to show her work, they needed prices. She had not even thought about selling her photographs, but friends and family loved them and wanted to purchase her work. Lynne did some research on what other artists charged for large pieces formatted on Plexiglas and factored in her costs. This helped her price her growing collection. Reaching out to local home and gift stores, Lynne was able to consign her pieces; they are selling, so she knows she's at the right price point.

On to Week 6, and I hope you are getting excited about your new venture—and the income it will bring you. Many women have a hard time asking to be paid for their service or product. Even women who are starting a business can feel awkward and ill at ease about asking for money. But if you are clear from the beginning, there will be no misunderstandings and you will be able to avoid uncomfortable situations.

WEEK 6 ASSIGNMENTS

Your goal this week is to come up with a pricing plan: you'll price your service or product and draft a clear, descriptive explanation of your pricing policy—one that leaves no room for confusion. You'll also create packages and samples to entice clients to buy. Time to pull out your Notebook and get started on getting paid for what you do.

Assignment #1: Research What Others Are Charging

Find out what others are charging for similar items or services. Pricing a product is a bit easier than a service because you know the cost of materials and can factor in your time, but you also need to be competitive and make sure clients feel they are getting a good value. Books have been written on how to price your product or service, but in my opinion, the easiest thing to do is to see what the market will bear in your area for your product or service, and then price accordingly.

Let's start with a service. Different services are priced depending on multiple factors; one of those factors is location. In some areas of the country an hour of someone's time costs more than it does in another part of the country for the same service. For example, in the Northeast, $125 an hour for a certain kind of service is not unreasonable; the same service in the Midwest would be priced at $75 an hour. Some services are priced by the job rather than by the hour. Decide if that makes sense for what you are offering. Look at what others are charging in your area for similar services. If your product or service is so unique that nothing else like it exists, ask potential clients what they would pay. (You might want to start with your friends.)

Here's an example. If you are offering to be a personal gift shopper for clients and your competitors charge $75 an hour, you don't want to price yourself at $250 an hour unless you can show you are worth it. In this case, maybe you'd charge a flat fee of $50 to shop for the item, send three choices by email, buy the gift once they have decided, wrap it, and deliver it to your client. In your description, be clear about how and when you will deliver the gift and what the wrapping will consist of. Outline that shipping is an additional charge, for example, "cost to ship to recipient is an additional $10 plus the cost of shipping."

If you are just starting your venture, I would recommend pricing a bit under your competition. You can always raise your rates later as demand grows. This is why it is important to research what is being charged in the area where you will offer your service and price accordingly.

List your competitors' charges in your Notebook. Find out how long they've been in business and make notes on how they charge for their services. Compare what you are offering and decide on your charge for the service or your hourly rate. If the competition's rates vary substantially, figure out what advantages are being offered with the higher pricing.

If you will be selling a product, hit the streets and search the Web. Go to the types of boutiques or stores that would carry your item for sale and make a note of prices. Look at comparable items and the details of how they are made or what they are made of. Handmade items are usually more expensive. Look at the cost of labor and materials needed to produce your own product, and set the price a certain percent above your cost. The storekeeper's markup for most fashion items, if that's what you plan to sell, is 100 percent, so make sure your price to the boutique is in line with other similar items for sale in your area.

It's important to make sure that you are selling your items through the Internet for the same price that boutiques are charging. Shop owners do not appreciate showcasing and stocking your item to then find out that shoppers saw it in their store and then went online to your e-commerce site to get a lower price. Usually you would offer a wholesale discount to shops and charge full price online.

As your business grows, other factors may enter into your pricing strategy. But for Week 6, thoroughly research the local competition and set your price.

 IN YOUR NOTEBOOK

If your business is a service, for each of your local competitors:

- List their prices.
- Note how long they've been in business.
- Identify any particular advantages they offer.
- Record how they charge for their services.

Compare your own offering with your competitors' offerings and set a price for your own service, either by project/service or by hourly rate. If your business is a product,

- Check out competitors' products at local retailers and online.
- Make a record of the prices for similar goods.
- Note the materials and workmanship of competitors' goods.

Calculate your own cost of labor and materials and price your products a certain percentage above that figure, in line with competitors' pricing. Whether you sell online, at boutiques, or in local markets, pricing should be uniform.

Assignment #2: Create and Price Packages

Offering a package—a group of products put together and priced below what it would cost to buy the items separately—can be a great way to build your client base.

By grouping products or services together you are able to sell more and use the package to entice buyers to spend more. Customers like packages because they are getting multiple items or services. And you can offer something free with a paid item to entice a new client to try you.

For example, if you are starting a wardrobe-styling venture, you might group several services together and offer a first-time package. If your hourly rate is $50, you might offer a beginning package with a free one-hour consultation at the person's home, a closet organization of two hours, and a two-hour shopping trip to the local mall, all for $185. That's a total of five hours, so the discount is $65—but you're still making $37 an hour and gaining a grateful repeat client who will mention you and your service to her friends.

When you are working to get your first clients or new clients, beginning packages work well. Your future marketing material will highlight this savings. And as you build relationships, you've made your ongoing clients aware of what you charge. When a past client hires you to prepare outfits for an upcoming wedding, graduation weekend, or season change, she'll know your work and that your rate is $50 an hour with a two-hour minimum.

By providing your product or service in a package, clients get a better deal and exposure to more of what you are offering. But be very specific about your time. If you're working as a wardrobe stylist, meet at the shopping location. Be clear with the client, "I'll meet you at the mall's entrance at 1:00 P.M. and we'll have until 3:00 P.M. to shop." Don't feel guilty about ending your session. If you are on a roll with a client and both of you want to continue shopping, be very clear. "Let me look at my schedule to see if I can give you another hour. The additional charge will be at my regular hourly rate of $50. Does that work for you?"

Another illustration would be a venture where you offer computer help. Be very specific about what you are offering. One mom I know offers password consolidation and automatic bill pay setup for a set price of $175. She gathers a client's passwords and logins and organizes them by category, delivering them to her client in an Excel spreadsheet. She also sets up logins and passwords for automatic bill pay for all of the client's service providers and utilities.

This is a service that is not defined by time but rather by the project. She has determined that most projects take approximately two hours, so she should add the caveat: "If your project takes more than two hours, there will be an additional charge of $25 per hour." As you can see, it's important that you have an accurate assessment of how much time you will need when you price a project.

If your venture is in the area of computer help, many of the services you offer can be combined into packages. All of these can be outlined on your website and clearly detailed in your marketing materials.

Packages build customer commitment. If you are providing family meals on Tuesdays and Thursdays, offer a set price for one—and a discount if they order for both nights. If you are planning to start a dog-walking service, give a bonus of an extra walk or two when clients hire you for a month. If you present the client with a bill, always list the bonus (with a nice "$0.00" in the price column) in the details of the bill.

If you have products that can be packaged together, great. Many single items, like jewelry or belts, can be packaged: you could offer a personal strap fitting when customers buy a belt or a creative bag to hold a necklace when they buy earrings too. Whether you have a product or service, create several packages or bonuses that give clients additional incentive to use you—and that give them a bit of a discount.

 IN YOUR NOTEBOOK

- Research your competitors' package offerings and take notes on what you see as advantages and disadvantages.
- Make a list of possible packages you could create from your own product or service offerings.
- Price your packages. Remember, the goal is to introduce the customer to the range of your products and services and provide a discount.

Assignment #3: Offer a Free Consultation or Sample

A great way to entice people to try your business and to build a relationship is to offer a free assessment or consultation. In the wardrobe-styling example, you might offer a free hour of wardrobe consulting. This could consist of having the client fill out a questionnaire that tells you what she has in her closet and what she needs in terms of clothing. You would then schedule an hour, by phone or in person, when you would discuss her needs, let her know how you can help her, how you work with most clients, and most importantly, what you charge. Leave the client with a list of additional services and follow up with an email with suggestions and needs that you discovered in your assessment. Be very clear about what is part of a free assessment and what will be a billable charge. You don't want any misunderstandings about how you price your services.

When a client says he or she would like to use you, you may consider getting a deposit up front. Assuming you're a wardrobe consultant, after the free assessment, and when the client hires you to help her get several outfits for her new job, you would prepare an invoice asking for a 50 percent deposit up front.

Finally, remember your time is money, so begin and end on time. One mom I know visibly sets an alarm on her phone when she begins so there is no confusion.

Find an enticement to garner new clients or to get current clients to purchase more of what you are offering. If you offer exercise classes or personal fitness, offer the first class free. If you are redesigning bookcases or doing color consulting, give a free in-home overview of what you can do to help them.

You're not able to offer a free consultation with a product, but you can find a way to offer something. If your business is selling beauty or food products, create small samples. Tasting and sampling a product gives customers comfort with their purchase. Find a way to offer some kind of bonus or discount that will entice customers. If you offer belt buckles and straps, offer a 10 percent discount on a strap when they buy a buckle. If you sell cookies, offer a free cookie of another type when they purchase a package of their favorite.

IN YOUR NOTEBOOK

For your product or service venture, list some possible opportunities for creating a free consultation or sample.

Assignment #4: Write a Clear Description of Your Fees

Be very clear about what your price or fee covers. For a service where you charge by the hour, outline the services provided and not provided and the minimum number of hours required. Make sure your client knows if you do, or do not, prorate partial hours. For a per-project fee, be clear that if the project takes more than a specific number of hours, there will be an hourly charge for the overage. For a product, make sure the client knows all of the specifics up front. Artists and photographers, for example, need to be clear about sizes, whether or not framing is included, and what kinds of frames and paper will be used.

Prepare a sample pricing sheet that outlines in detail what you are providing. For example, "ABC Clothing Consultants will spend two hours shopping with you at the XYZ Mall on a mutually decided date and time for $___. Additional hours will be billed $___/hour." If your service involves delivering a finished product for which you charge by the job, describe what you will deliver and when. If your service is providing family meals, you might say in your pricing sheet and marketing, "Each meal consists of a main course, two side dishes, and bread to serve five, and will be delivered by 5:00 P.M. on the designated day. Cost is $65.00. Payment in cash is expected at time of delivery." Organize things so that when you get an order, you'll be prepared to send an email confirmation of your fees and how you expect to be paid. If you create an invoice, simply charge according to the fees you outlined in your pricing sheet. Have an invoice template ready to go.

IN YOUR NOTEBOOK

Using the information you gathered in the previous four assignments, prepare a pricing sheet and an invoice template so you'll be ready to go when orders come in.

Here are some examples of pricing descriptions. First from a wardrobe consultant:

ABC WARDROBE CONSULTING

30-minute closet assessment — free

2-hour closet clean-out — $195, each additional hour $80

2-hour shopping trip — $195, each additional hour $80

Wardrobe plan for a trip — $95 per hour

Closet Clean-Out and Shopping Trip Special — $350 (a $40 savings)

* * * *

Payment by cash or check is expected at time of service.

Partial hours are prorated.

And from a photo-book business:

ALL THINGS PHOTO: BOOKS AND ORGANIZING

All Things Photo is here to create coffee table books using the photos from your life. Whether it's the year in the life of your family or a special occasion book, we'll do everything. Here is the simple step by step process.

1. Download your photos to Shutterfly.
2. Choose the size book you'd like and the number of pages from the pricing below. Send us payment via the PayPal link on our site. Add the additional fee for captions if you'd like them.

	10" x 10"	10" x 12.5"	12" x 12"	Add captions (per book)
26 pages	$100	$125	$150	$25
38 pages	$150	$175	$200	$35
50 pages	$200	$225	$275	$45
76 pages	$275	$300	$325	$70

3. Share your photos with us on Shutterfly.

We'll do the rest. Look for a copy via email to proof within three weeks. Email us any edits. Once we receive your edits, the book will be delivered to you. All orders are final, but we feel confident you'll love your photo book.

Any questions? Contact Maia at: www.allthingsphoto.com

Be very specific about how the process works and what a client will be charged. You should be equally specific when describing your prices and your policies about cancellations, returns, and methods of payment.

If you are selling a product online on your own website, clearly outline the prices, taxes, and shipping costs. Brick-and-mortar stores and other online stores can sell your product for you as well. When working with a shop or online store that is reselling your items, be sure to get an agreement in writing that details their commission and any additional charges.

If you are leaving things with a store on consignment, make a list of what you are leaving and get the shopkeeper to sign off on it. Include full descriptions and prices. Outline any contingencies for discounting. For example, the store may get an offer lower than your marked price. Either give them your lowest price, ask them to call you with any offer lower than the marked price, or tell them there is no negotiation.

If for some reason you do not get paid in a timely manner, send a reminder email. If that doesn't result in payment, a phone call may be in order. Remember it's all in the delivery of your message. "I'm sure you are so busy, but I'm working to close out my accounting from last month and was hoping to get final payment from you by the end of the week. I'll email an invoice now in case you lost my last one. I can come by and pick up a check if necessary." Be sure to give people the benefit of the doubt. Most clients have every intention of paying; they just may need a reminder.

You need a plan for how to handle returns on a product or to placate an unhappy customer. Your return policy should be clearly outlined. For a product, will you offer a full refund, including shipping, or will you offer a credit only? Either is fine, but be clear so that you can point to a stated policy on your website or invoice.

For service businesses, dealing with an unhappy or unsatisfied customer can be a bit trickier. Offering complete satisfaction by giving more time can garner new clients and happiness from current clients. But don't spend too much time trying to fix a problem that can't be fixed, no matter how much time you spend on it. If you find you have spent more than twice the usual time to fix a situation, work to end the relationship amicably. If someone is truly unhappy, the best policy is to take the high road and give them a refund with a letter of apology.

Feedback from an unhappy customer can be extremely helpful in dealing with future customers, so be open to hearing what they have to say. When you set up your website in Week 7, you can add a payment product like PayPal and a shopping cart to make it easier for your clients to pay you.

Now is the time to get started pricing your service or product and drafting the specific details of how you charge, what you charge, and how a client can pay you. (You will also use these details in your marketing materials, which we'll begin work on in Week 8.)

In the following stories, see how other moms have priced their products and services.

PRICING SUCCESS STORIES

Although these venture moms offer very different products and services, what they each have is a well-thought-out plan and a good pricing strategy. Will some modification of any of these work for you?

Unbakeables: Julie and Corey Tolkin

Who doesn't love cookie dough? When her kids were young, Julie would let them eat some of the dough from her cookies but worried about the raw eggs in the dough. So she and her sister decided it was a "culinary challenge" to create a cookie dough that was safe—and would be loved by children. And they succeeded! Not only with their own children, but throughout the neighborhood.

Fast-forward 20 years and Julie's daughter Corey has just graduated with a master's in education. "Corey said to me that she wanted to try a cooking venture before she started her teaching career." So this mother and daughter began to think about what they could do in the food realm, and were thinking of catering. They reached out to the local Score chapter, an organization that helps start-ups develop a plan. Julie says, "They told us our business would have to be unique and focused in order to succeed. We decided catering wasn't it."

They thought about what would fit the bill and remembered their success with cookie dough. Corey and Julie set out to develop several flavors and worked with ways to package the dough. At a family dinner discussing their idea, they came up with the plan to package bite-size discs of dough in a plastic sleeve. Each disc of dough is covered in something to separate them, like sprinkles for the sugar cookie dough or chocolate for the chocolate chip cookie dough. Now they needed a name. Julie's youngest son came up with "Unbakeables."

Before selling at a local farmers' market, the two worked to make larger batches. They tested and perfected their recipe, got a license, found a commercial kitchen, designed their own labels, and self-funded everything. "This is truly a family start-up." Julie and Corey did some research and worked backwards using the cost to produce each unit to come up with a price that would entice buyers and also give them a profit.

After a few months Julie and Corey were ready to approach a local grocery store. Peters Market has been in Weston for years and the owner knew the Tolkins. "The owner saw an article in the local paper on the treat. When I reached out to him with a test batch, he said, 'I know you, and I'm sure your Unbakables are great.' He told us to bring in a few varieties to go on shelves immediately." They came up with a wholesale pricing structure that would work.

That was in February 2012. The coveted treat is now in many local stores and even Whole Foods. "We would just walk into specialty markets with samples and our fact sheet and ask if they would be willing to carry our product. For Whole Foods, we filled out an application and got accepted."

When asked where they want to go next, the two say, "Who knows, we're just taking one step at a time and we'll see where we end up."

The Cooking Fairy: Joanna Wallis

What would a busy mom in Fairfield County, Connecticut, pay to have a healthy home-cooked meal waiting in her refrigerator to be reheated when she gets home from carpooling at 6:00 with three starving children? That's what Joanna Wallis had to figure out when others offered to pay her to cook for them. And she discovered that by packaging several nights together she got more business. Pricing was instrumental in her success.

It's 3:00 P.M. and in addition to taking your oldest to an orthodontist appointment while dropping your middle at ballet class and your youngest at the soccer field, your dog needs to go to the vet and *then* you have to circle back and pick everyone up from their activities. You arrive home at 6:00 P.M. and realize there is no dinner. But wait, you open your fridge and there is a fabulous three-course meal ready to be popped in the oven for thirty minutes at 350°, according to the carefully explicit instructions taped to the top of the package. The Cooking Fairy was here.

Joanna Wallis left her sales job in software to stay at home with her three kids, but when her youngest finally started preschool, Joanna thought about what she wanted to do. It had to be a nine-to-three job with flexibility. "Family meals are so important; my own mother made it a habit. I was a really good cook, so why not do something around that?"

Her friends always complained that they never had time to make a good meal because they were so busy running their kids around in the afternoons. For Joanna, family dinner time was the best time of the day with her kids. "Not only does it encourage good eating habits, but it also teaches conversational skills. So if I could help other families with healthy meal preparation, I'd be offering a great service."

In 2010, Joanna started with a few families as clients. "I'd take all the ingredients and all of my pots and pans to different houses and prepare the meal for the night. At one point I was cooking for two or three families a day." She initially priced her meals based on the ingredients she used and the time it took to prepare them. This was a custom service, and Joanna's customer base was limited to the number of families she could cook for in a day. She found that she had to say no to some requests for her service.

As her business grew, Joanna realized that she needed to have a central place from which to prepare meals. This would allow her to provide meals for more families. She found a catering company that let her rent kitchen space during the day. There she was able to prepare meals for all her clients. Because she was preparing different meals for each family, this was a much more efficient arrangement, and she was able to expand her customer base. Delivery is a part of her service: she leaves the prepared meals in casserole dishes in her clients' refrigerators so when they get home, dinner is there.

Joanna sends out menus via email a few days in advance and takes orders. Knowing ahead of time what ingredients she'll need, she can buy in bulk and save money. This approach—posting menus and taking orders—enables Joanna to set a price for a meal rather than varying her price for cooking at someone's home.

Profitable from the beginning, Joanna wants to build on her concept. "I hear such great feedback from my clients. It's quite satisfying to know I'm helping families have more time together."

Who is her target market? Families with multiple kids in several activities, working parents, and people who don't cook either because they don't know how or don't have time. And she herself is done by 3:00 P.M. every day so she can go home and be with her children who are 8, 10, and 11.

One client said to Joanna, "I don't know what I would do without you. We'd probably be having takeout every night." According to Joanna, "It's tremendously satisfying to know I built a business on my own terms."

TAKEAWAY

- Set a price based on your research and feedback from potential clients (provided it gives you ample profit margins).
- Find a way to scale your venture to generate more income in the same amount of time. By consolidating, Joanna was able to provide more meals and create more income.

Taylor Home: Carolyn Taylor

Carolyn Taylor wanted a job where she could do what she loved all the time and get paid to do it. She loves to shop for cool and unusual home décor items at tag sales, flea markets, and antique malls. She found a way to get paid to shop when she began offering the service of bookcase styling on an hourly basis with a two-hour minimum.

She starts there and can move on to accessorizing a client's entire home.

Her tiny college dorm room was the place that her girlfriends wanted to be. With its roman shades, hand-sewn duvet, and coordinated rug, Carolyn Taylor had created a happy space for herself and her classmates to enjoy. Her love of finishing spaces continued when she started a family. She honed her skills with her own home as she transformed a historic colonial and gave it a modern twist with her own style.

Carolyn's goal was to create a venture where she could get paid to do what she loved. When friends and family expressed their love of Carolyn's creative style in her home, they also began to ask her to help with their own decorating projects. Starting with bookcases, Carolyn offered to rearrange collectables and books in a way that showcased the homeowner's individual style. Her hourly rate for this service is $100. She determined this based on what interior designers charge in her area for an hour of their time.

She became known as the woman who could create a fabulous bookcase look. "I found that once I was working in a client's home on a bookcase, they would want me to do more things, like fireplace mantles and tabletop tableaus." Carolyn would simply repurpose what the homeowner had and make suggestions for a few additional items. When the home-owner asked her to shop for those finishing touches, she realized that she could do that as well on an hourly basis. This led her to offer a decorating finishing service. The rate is the same as for her bookcase styling service, but there is a two-hour minimum. She would shop for things like pillows, throws, and small accessories. She had found a way to get paid to do what she loved.

Carolyn will also work with a client remotely, online. For example, she can sit in front of the computer and design a room in about two hours using things from IKEA, CB2, and Pottery Barn. For this service the rate is $200 an hour for a specific project.

Although she doesn't have a website or a written price structure, she outlines the following when a client asks to work with her and she collects a check after she completes the project. Because all of her clients come through word of mouth or referrals from friends, she feels comfortable with a verbal price quote.

Assessment and walk-through at your home for an hour — Free
Bookcase styling — $100 an hour
Personal shopping for finishing touches — $100 an hour with a two-hour minimum
Room finishing and paint color consultation — $100 an hour with a two-hour minimum

She has realized that her specialty is in finding finishing touches, find-ing and styling things like lamps, books, coral pieces, and boxes, all of the things that make a room feel lived in and loved. She doesn't add charges to items she sources, but can negotiate discounts for her clients at places she frequents. Her payment is for the time she spends shopping. "Style has no price tag. I can help people display their own style on whatever budget."

According to Carolyn, "editing" is key. "Sometimes by taking things out, I can give a room a new feel. I don't want to be a decorator searching for fabrics, but rather an accessory gal. Ultimately, the client is in charge of the amount of time, energy, and money they dedicate to a project."

TAKEAWAY

- When charging by the hour, research the current hourly rate in your area for what you provide.
- Set a minimum number of hours for your service.

Off to Dreamland: Sasha Carr

Sasha Carr was looking for more flexibility with her work when she became a mom. Sleep consulting seemed like the perfect addition to her therapy practice and it would give her more independence.

She had been a psychologist for many years, but her baby's playgroup led her to a new venture. Sasha Carr was a full-time therapist with a doctorate in clinical psychology when she had her son. "When I became a mom myself, I saw a lot of misery over the little sleep so many new moms were getting, myself included." This is when Sasha learned about the field of sleep consulting.

Sasha says, "I had every intention of going back to my therapy practice but I wanted something with more flexibility and where I wouldn't be tied to an office." She heard about the Family Sleep Institute and researched what they were offering. The center trained people to assist parents in getting their children to sleep on a regular schedule. She signed up for the course, which was an intensive program that included hands-on supervision.

During this time, she was still managing her own therapy practice but once trained, she set out to name, price, brand, and market her new venture. This included setting up a website and social media. Sasha reached her target audience by aligning with a local pediatric office where she gave talks to new mothers on establishing good sleep habits for their children.

"I offer several programs for children ages four months to five years that have very close to a hundred percent success rate. So after two weeks I've worked myself out of a job," she told me. But it turned out that so many parents needed Sasha's help, she was able to scale down her therapy practice and focus exclusively on sleep coaching.

Her new venture's name is Off to Dreamland. On her website she describes in detail what is included in each package and lists the prices. But rather than having a payment link right on her website, prospective clients must call or fill out a contact form. "I like to discuss the issues and make sure we are a good fit to work together." Then she sends a link to pay via PayPal and an extensive questionnaire for parents to complete and send back to her. "This guides me in setting up a plan for the parents to implement over the next two weeks."

Sasha starts with an hour-long session by phone or in person. She is available during the two weeks to talk with the parents and walk them through any issues by phone or email. "Some clients need a lot of intensive support while others only check in once or twice." She says when a client calls, they are usually at their wits' end and need help *yesterday*. "My job is to come up with a specialized plan for the child and empower the parents to implement it."

And she's working on a children's book that encourages good sleep habits. The inspiration came when a young client began "teaching" her teddy bear good sleep habits. She suggests this technique in her coaching. Using that as a base, her book is about a little boy who helps a monkey get good sleep.

Sasha is not at a loss for clients, working with about 20 clients a month, and she feels good that she is doing something that makes a difference in people's lives. Most of her business comes from pediatrician's offices and word of mouth.

TAKEAWAY

- Clearly outline what is included in each service or package you offer.
- Give potential customers an email and phone number for contact if there is not a payment option on your site.
- Set up a PayPal account for ease of payment.

———

Pricing is critically important to your venture. Before you tell the world what you are doing, have a very clear pricing plan in place. And next, in Week 7, you'll put it on the website you're going to set up.

seven

Week 7:
Take It to the Web

When Pam Pik started her college consulting business, she knew one of the first things she needed was a website where potential clients could read about the services she would provide and find information about her background and experience. She started with the basics and over time added a blog and an "Ask Pam" feature. But in the beginning, she started with a basic Web presence where college-bound students and their parents could find her. The rest came later.

Don't let the idea of creating a website scare you. A website is essential for doing business today, even if you have nothing more than your contact information on a home page. Getting your venture to the Web should be at the top of your to-do list, and you can get it done this week.

WEEK 7 ASSIGNMENTS

Go live with your site. Setting up a website can be as easy or as difficult as you want to make it, but it has to be up this week, no matter how scant. You will add to your site as you go.

Assignment #1: Choose a Hosting Site and Secure Your Domain

Go to one of the many hosting sites on the Web and secure your domain (if you didn't already do so when you named your venture, back in Chapter 4). If your first choice is not available, come up with an alternative. For example, if your venture is called Cakes by Pam and www.cakesbypam. com is taken, consider adding your state or town, as in www.CakesbyPam-Seattle.com. Other things to add to the domain would be "llc," "4you," your state, your zip code, or a significant number. Try shortening your name if your full name is taken, or try adding a period or dash between words or letters.

You can find many sites that offer hosting for anywhere from $2 to $20 a month. Some that I like are NetworkSolutions.com, HostGator.com, BlueHost.com, and GoDaddy.com. A variety of standard templates are available for your use on most of these sites. There may be a fee. Try to find a template that matches or coordinates with your colors and style. This is the easy way to get up and running.

Each of these services will walk you through the process of creating a basic website. Even if you've never done much technical work before, you can put up a simple website by choosing one of their templates and go live in about an hour. And you'll be able to update it yourself. Many of these hosting sites offer online or live help to get you started. (For a list of hosting sites, see the Resources section at the end of this book.)

While you can do extensive research on setting up a website, I want you to cut to the chase and get yours up and running. The goal is to have a place to refer people to when they ask what you do or ask you for information about your product or service. It doesn't have to be perfect; it just has to be.

When you're ready to go beyond the basics, you can brand your site by putting a "skin" on it. A skin is the overlay of your colors and style on top of the content. This can be an exciting step, and you'll find numerous Web designers at all price points who can help you with this. With careful research it's possible to find a designer who can help you brand your site in a short period of time for a minimal cost (somewhere between $100 and $1,000). So do your research, but don't let this stop you from getting a basic site up using a standard template from one of the hosting services mentioned above.

IN YOUR NOTEBOOK

- Decide which hosting site you plan to use.
- When you're ready to move beyond the basics on your website, research Web design resources and make a list of possible choices.

Assignment #2: Research Other Sites

Back to the Internet for more research. The first thing you want to know is what do others who do what you do or sell what you sell have on their websites. Keep a list of sites you like in your Notebook for reference. Keep a list of features you like as well. The second thing you want to learn is more general: look at sites that have nothing to do with your venture just to get ideas on structure and layout. What do they have in their navigation bar that you want in yours?

Most sites have *Home, About,* and *Contact.* You'll also want *Shop* if you are offering products and services that can be bought online.

A basic navigation bar will have the following:

- **Home**: Your logo and a brief description of what you are offering. This is where you tell potential clients and customers how you can help them and why they should choose you.
- **About**: Who you are and what your qualifications are; a history of you and your firm. Keep this light and focused on your venture. This is the place to tell why you are doing what you are doing. This is not the place to put your resumé. If your schooling is important to your venture, it makes sense to include that information, but otherwise focus on your passion for your venture and why and how you got started. This section should be between 200 and 400 words.
- **Contact**: Name, email, and phone number (your physical address may not be necessary).
- **Products** or **Shop**: Photos, descriptions, and prices. Even if you don't have a shopping cart, you should include photos of your products. If you offer a service, provide some photos of yourself providing the service. Before and after photos are a great idea for showcasing what you do. (If you are planning to sell items online, setting up a shopping cart may take longer to implement. Sites like

Shopify.com can help you get started. But get the basic site up this week; you can always add a shopping cart later.)

- **FAQs**: Frequently Asked Questions (FAQs) is one of the most important links to have in your navigation bar. This is your opportunity to shine. This is where you get to tell users what you do and how you can help them. Look at websites for similar products or services and use the FAQs they have posted as a model; answer the same questions for your venture. Think of every question a user might have and put this in your FAQs. You want the user to be able to get information on your venture readily and find the site easy to navigate. The FAQs will explain to the user how to use the site to meet their needs. Ask a friend who is unfamiliar with your venture to ask you questions about your product or service and incorporate those into this link.

When you think about what to put on your site and in your navigation bar, think about how other ventures have structured their navigation bars. What do you like about the sites you frequent?

 IN YOUR NOTEBOOK

- Research as many sites as you can for ventures that offer products or services similar to yours. Make notes about your favorite sites and your favorite features.
- Research sites that interest you but have no connection whatsoever to your venture. Make a list of the structure, layout, and features that you like on these sites.
- Research and list items for your FAQs.
- Take notes on well-designed navigation bars on other sites.

Assignment #3: Go Live with Your Site

Even if you only get one page up with your contact information and your logo, do it this week. You can add more details and pages later. And you can look for help if you need it. But this is the week to go live with your site.

If and when you decide you need help expanding your site and adding other features, there are many ways to get help. Several women I've talked with have had help from their teenage children. One teenage girl was able to set up a storefront and shopping cart for her mom's budding fashion line. Keep in mind that many of the hosting services can walk you through the process at no charge or will provide step-by-step instructions.

Congratulations! You're ready to market your venture. You've come up with a great name. You have colors that speak to who you are and what your venture is. You've set up a clear pricing structure so your clients know what your product or service costs and how to pay you.

WEBSITE SUCCESS STORIES

Your website is live and telling potential clients and customers who you are, what you do, what you charge, and how to reach you. Now you're ready to put it out there. See how the moms profiled below set up their websites, and then get started on yours.

Good Gardens: Karen Hughan

When Karen Hughan wanted to announce to the world that she was providing landscape design services, it was her daughter who helped her put together a website with her contact information and pictures of her own garden. As her business grew, she was able to add photos of the jobs she had designed and installed. Her site is a simple informational site where potential clients can see her work and get her contact and background information. Since her site really functions as a resumé and portfolio, she doesn't need a shopping cart, but her contact information is imperative.

The seeds of Karen Hughan's career were planted when she was a child, helping her grandmother and her father, who were avid gardeners, plant flowers and vegetables each spring. After getting a degree in horticulture and natural resources, she found her first job in interior landscaping, where she provided plantings and gardens for malls, atria, and office buildings. During this time, while on a business trip in California when her daughters were five and nine, she counted the number of full weeks that year that she had been home: 14. Her friend remembers her sobbing while she tried to figure out how she could spend less time traveling for work and more time at home.

Karen ultimately left her job to be at home, but once her two girls were in high school she found that she missed the process of landscape design. When one of Karen's friends asked her to add and manage a garden section to her home goods store in town, she jumped at the chance.

While she worked in the shop for just a year, the exposure it offered allowed her to build her gardening reputation with local customers. It was a natural transition from this role to her own business providing home garden design. Through word of mouth jobs began to trickle in.

But designing gardens wasn't enough to fill the year. Drafting designs usually happens during the winter months, and Karen needed to fill the other times of the year with work. Her entrepreneurial intuition led her to diversify her services based on the seasons. Karen provides container and window box planting in the early spring. The summer is for installation, often moving a client's existing plants so she can stay within an allotted budget. In late fall, she decorates clients' homes for the holidays, working with a homeowner's vases, containers, and family pieces. All this is shown on her website, so clients know she can provide these services as well as garden design. Karen has created a full-time job for herself, but on a schedule of her own making.

Karen's older daughter has entered the entrepreneurial world as well by starting her own Web design business; she designed her mom's website. Karen is happy to see her daughter has inherited her entrepreneurial spirit.

Karen's business has grown to the point that she's considering moving her operations from her home and garage into a storefront of her own. Her steady, creative approach to building her business, helped by the right Internet strategy, has sown the seeds for growth.

TAKEAWAY

- Start simple. See if your children can help you set up a basic website—one page with your contact information. This may be all you need to get started.
- If you have a service venture like Karen's, start with photos of your current work, as she did with pictures from her home landscaping. Then add photos as you add to your portfolio.
- As you add different services, add them to your site.

Henri's Reserve: Ruth Frantz

*When you have a service or product line that requires explanation, edu-
cation, and a shopping cart with size choices, you'll probably need some
help to get your site ready. This was the case with Henri's Reserve, a
vendor of boutique champagnes. The site not only explains to users what
boutique champagnes are, but also presents options for purchasing cases,
gift packages, and various groupings of these wines. Ruth Frantz has
created a site that epitomizes the celebratory nature of champagne.*

Two years ago, when someone asked her where she lived, she replied, "The
British Airways Airport Lounge." With a 10-year-old, Ruth Frantz wanted
to create a career where she wouldn't have to travel so much and could
work from anywhere with just a laptop and cell phone. So she took a leap
and quit her corporate job to restructure her life, even though she had no
idea what she would do.

Ruth's corporate job involved building brands for a spirits company,
working specifically on champagne. While thinking about her next move,
she had a pivotal conversation with a friend about the fabulous artisanal
family-estate champagnes that were nearly impossible to find in the United
States. This gave her an idea. She knew there were hundreds of small win-
eries in the champagne region of France that produce small quantities of
high-quality champagnes. "I decided to offer these boutique champagnes
via e-commerce." As an experienced at-home hostess with a deep knowledge of food and wines, marketing champagne was a natural extension of
her talents and interests.

Ruth knew how to build new products and spirits brands, and navigat-
ing the legal requirements for importing alcohol products was like a second language to her. She needed a name and an image for her new idea,
and she envisioned a sophisticated but warm Frenchman guiding champagne lovers around the vineyards of France. An amalgamation of old
friends and acquaintances became the Henri you see on her site, drawn by
a professional illustrator. The collection of champagnes became "the reserve," *et voilà*—Henri's Reserve was born.

Ruth sought help from a friend to develop her presence on the Web,
with excellent results. Her site not only introduces visitors to the world of
artisanal champagnes, it also encourages them to think of champagne in a
variety of new ways: as a memorable gift, as an accompaniment to unex-

pected foods, and as the centerpiece for a special celebration. Through her site, Ruth offers a concierge service for those seeking expert help in making a gift of these artisanal champagnes. "I saw a niche that wasn't being filled. Using my past experience and skill set, I was able to start my own thing."

How does Ruth market her product? "That's the fun part. The minute you pop a bottle of champagne, everything is transformed." Ruth uses a combination of social media, PR, events, and tastings to market these specialty champagnes. Since her business is all e-commerce, she utilizes a warehouse and fulfillment center. With growth in mind for Henri's Reserve, Ruth has partnered with other brands, including Vosges Haut-Chocolat, to offer combination packages. Ruth says, "In life and career, you have to be able to pivot," and she has pivoted to a cool and unique business idea.

TAKEAWAY

- Create your business around something that taps both your experience and your passion.
- Whenever possible, enlist a friend with the right experience to help with a technical project. Barter with friends if you can.
- Look for partnering opportunities to showcase your products.

The EDWIN: Candice Frankel

Designing your website to look like the product you're selling is a cool idea that Candice Frankel used with her educational product. The EDWIN is a folder for helping high school students get organized and ready for the college application process. When you open The EDWIN website, it looks like the product. Candice uses PayPal as her shopping cart, which she says was not difficult to set up. "Many moms aren't into the PayPal world yet, but soon will be, it's so easy."

Many times your past career will lead you directly to your own venture. That's what happened with Candice Frankel. She had been a college counselor to high school students for 20 years before going out on her own to offer guidance privately through her own firm. During her time in the field, Candice had developed a system—and a product—for the students she worked with. "I saw that students needed to begin to get organized as early as ninth grade. I felt that if they were waiting until junior year, they might miss out on key opportunities for figuring out what kind of college would be the best fit for them."

The organizational tool Candice developed, called "The EDWIN," short for Educational Winners, is designed to help kids organize and store essential documents and important papers, helping them to build skills that will not only help them in the runup to college applications but long after. She originally intended to use her system for her own clients. However, when the private school where she had worked bought The EDWIN for each of their ninth graders, she realized there was a market for her product—one that would enable her to reach a much broader audience. She also realized that in order to offer her product to this broader audience, she would need a website.

So she got to work. In developing her product for sale, she wrote content, sourced the perfect folder, and hired a graphic designer who could see and translate her vision for the product. The process took three months, and she had to work through a couple of prototypes before finding a manufacturer who could create the functionality and look she wanted and be cost-effective at the same time. Her website is organized to look and function like her product—the classic file folder. Its simple design underscores the thoughtful, comprehensive approach she takes to the college admissions process.

She began marketing The EDWIN to friends who had children in high school. "The feedback was overwhelmingly positive. It felt so satisfying to see my concept come to fruition." She was then ready to roll it out to a broader audience. She began with an e-commerce website that she set up herself. She branded her site with her logo, and the look of the actual folder shows potential clients and customers what her product is and what it can do for them.

Candice's two girls are 10 and 12 and are very proud of their mom. They say they can't wait to use The EDWIN themselves. Candice says, "Developing a product and building a business around it has been a great learning experience for me. I'm using my brain in a different way and I feel challenged every day."

TAKEAWAY

- Candice already had a product to market when she ventured out into her own business. Recognize if you have the same or can create it from work you are already doing.
- If possible, create a product that complements your service. Candice's paper product complements her college counseling service.

In these past four weeks you've named, priced, and branded your venture and launched your website. Marketing is up next.

III

PUT IT OUT
THERE

eight

Week 8:
Tell the World

You can actually launch a successful venture with one email. That's how Dawn Decosta got started. Working at the Apple Store didn't give her the flexibility she wanted, but she acquired the skills to help others with Apple products. Wondering how she could make teaching computer skills into a business, Dawn decided, "Do what I love, the money will follow." And it did. She sent out an email to her friends and family, and word of mouth spread about her teaching services. In a few weeks, clients were calling. When asked about the profile of most of her clients, she says seniors reach out to her a lot. "They didn't grow up with computers the way kids today have, and they need help one on one." She now teaches group classes at the local Parks and Recreation locations. "I taught Facebook and Twitter to four women at their kitchen table in an hour and a half." But Dawn is just at the beginning of her venture; as she points out, "I don't have a website and I haven't advertised yet." But this didn't stop her from getting started. It all began with one email.

This week we begin the marketing process. You may have the greatest product or service in the world, but if no one knows about it, it won't be successful. So put it out there.

With one email you can start a business, and with today's technology it's easy to stay in touch with your clients and followers. Many moms with their own ventures were up and running after one email went out to their friends and family, and some got their first clients this way, simply by telling people what they were offering. It can be that simple. This is the easiest way to market and build your following.

WEEK 8 ASSIGNMENTS

This week we'll look at the most effective ways to get the word out about your venture and the most effective ways to define your market.

Assignment #1: Create a Business Email Account

Create a specific email that is separate from your personal email. This step is part of making your venture look like the professional undertaking that it is. For example, info@cakesbypam.com or cakesbypam@gmail.com. Email accounts usually come with your Web-hosting packages, but you can also use gmail—it's free and easy to use. Create an email account using the name of your venture or a combination of your name and your venture's name: for example, HollyHurdVentureMom@gmail.com. And be sure to include all your social media accounts in your email signature. Here's an example: "Visit our website/Read our blog/Follow us on Twitter/Fan us on Facebook."

Let's look at what makes a good introduction. Your goal is to become known to someone who hasn't a clue who you are and doesn't have any idea of your abilities, skills, talents, products, and/or services. Follow the plan below to create your introductory email.

Include the following:

- Mention how friends and family have valued or admired your product or service.
- State the product or service you are offering.
- Tell where or how you will be offering the product or service.
- Invite people to view your product (attach some photos to the email). If you're offering a service, ask them to read more about it on your website.
- Ask them to spread the word to others.
- Ask them to add your new business email to their address book so they can get updates from you.
- Finish with your contact info and Web address.

Here are two sample introductory emails:

For a product:

Hi guys:

You've all admired my belt buckles for years, and now I'm turning my hobby into a business venture and offering you the chance to buy your own. Please visit my website, barbsbeltbuckles.com, or email me at barb@ barbsbeltbuckles.com for more information. I'm working to place my creative belt buckles in local shops, so if you have contacts or ideas, please send them along. And spread the word to your network. The current buckles are seen below with prices. New buckles can be seen on the site as well.

Place your orders now by emailing me directly. And please add my new business email to your address list so you get all of my updates.

For a service:

Hi everyone:

For years I've been restyling your homes using what you already have, and now I'm turning the skill I love to share into a business venture. If you know anyone who would like me to restyle their home, please pass along my contact information. I'm offering two hours of restyling and staging for an introductory rate of $195. Visit my website for before and after photos and more info at susiesdesign.com. I'm offering a free half-hour assessment. Please add my new business email to your address list so you get all of my updates.

SusieStyle@susiesdesign.com.

It's as simple as that. But be sure to use BCC (blind copy) for your contacts. To do this, put your email address in the "to" box and then click on "BCC" to insert all other contacts. That way, no one will see who you are sending to. It's important to respect the privacy of members of your group by hiding their addresses under BCC.

Assignment #2: Send an Email to Friends and Family

Draft an informative but short email and send it to everyone on your list. Use your new email address and ask recipients to add it to their address book so your future emails won't go to spam. Add a photo for both product and service ventures.

This is the time to start a list of email addresses of interested followers. In the next assignment, you'll see why this is important. First, let's take a look at something you'll come to rely on for putting it out there: an email marketing service provider.

You'll want to set up an email service account with an email marketing service provider. This account keeps track of parties interested in your venture and helps you manage your email marketing campaign.

Here's how it works: On your website, you'll offer users a chance to sign up to get updates on your venture. This will allow you to stay in touch about sales, new shops where your product can be found, news about you and your service, updates about your venture, and other content that engages your followers. Your site will link to your provider, where new contacts will be saved when they sign up. Setting this up may require help, and most providers can walk you through the process.

By using i-Contact, Constant Contact, MailChimp, or another email service, you can collect email addresses of people who want to receive information about your product or service. These email services can be free or may charge a monthly or yearly fee, some based on the number of contacts you have, some based on the number of emails you send out. A list of email marketing service providers can be found in the Resources section at the end of this book.

With each of these Web services, you can use a template to draft your initial e-letter and subsequent newsletters or customize a template with your colors, logo, and tag line. I'd suggest the latter. If you need help with this, a graphic or Web designer can help for a reasonable fee; better yet if you can barter your product or service.

You can create specific lists to help you target specific groups. To begin, you would definitely want a list of current clients whom you can update on a regular basis. And then you'd want a list of potential clients for other types of promotions to get them to become clients. You can delineate even further, depending on your needs. Other lists to start would be a list of press contacts or bloggers who you want to update with any news, developments, or special offers.

Assignment #3: Start an Email Marketing Service Account

Choose a provider you like and begin to collect email addresses of parties interested in your venture. Start by adding the friends and family who received your initial email and anyone else you've added. Let them know you'll be sending them updates on your venture in the form of a newsletter. Anyone that you add to the list must allow you to email them, and you should send a confirmation subscription notice when you add an email to your list. If large numbers of people report your email as spam, the provider has the right to bar you from using their service, so only add emails of people who give you permission. (Getting permission is required by law under "best practices" for sending blast emails.) You can set up a confirmation email that will go out automatically when someone signs up through your account.

Assignment #4: Draft Your First E-letter

Now you're ready to draft your initial e-letter, a newsletter you'll send through your email marketing service. Your first e-letter to the broader list should be an introductory letter. This may seem redundant, considering the email you sent to friends and family, but you're now showing your commitment to your venture by sending a polished e-letter from a source other than your email.

You'll want to steer clear of sending a weekly sales pitch, and this means you'll need to come up with content your users want to read. Include the same points that you included in your introductory email but in a more bullet-point fashion, and include your logo. The other difference is that you're adding relevant content.

Here are some important e-letter guidelines.

* Provide content that your followers will look forward to seeing.
* Plan to email at least once a month in the beginning.
* Keep your e-letters under 500 words—and include photos.
* Start each e-letter with something that pertains to what you are offering.

For example, if you're selling a fashion accessory, show an outfit with your item. If you're providing a service, show before and after photos or show a satisfied client. (Be sure to get permission from the clients before sending their photo to your followers.) Add a quote about what you do: "Studies show that a well-exercised dog is a happier dog." "People who live in an organized environment are happier." "The new trend in jewelry is gemstones."

Your love and enthusiasm for your venture will provide ideas for content. Stories about happy clients are always a good place to start. If you are a photo-book organizer, showcase a book you put together for someone's 90th birthday. If you are selling a food product, include photos of the item—along with a satisfied consumer. If you offer a pet product, show a different pet using your product in each letter. The possibilities are endless. Keep ideas in your Notebook.

Plan to email to your list at least once a month. The goal is to stay in touch with clients so they keep you and your product or service in their minds.

Here are some other content ideas: If you are a nutrition coach, send advice on digestive issues and include recipes in each letter. If you provide catering, send a letter suggesting meal ideas for families. If you are a personal trainer, describe a specific exercise. If you have a product, write about the experience of a satisfied purchaser or a new use for your product. You get the idea.

For informational letters designed to keep you in your target audience's mind, I would not send more than one a week. This is not a blog, but a way to keep in touch with your clients and potential clients.

You want to make sure your list of recipients opens your letter with anticipation. Send informative tips and suggestions around your expertise. Statistical data within your area of interest is another example of useful information. For example, a dog walker might send some statistics on how a dog that has been socialized with other dogs is a better-behaved dog. A personal trainer could send information on how exercise helps with bone strength. You can also include links to articles on subjects your audience will want to read. Write about clients you have helped. (Make sure you clear it with the client first.) Gather more ideas by looking at what others have put in their e-letters.

In these communications, you have the choice of being personal or not. This means that you can talk about yourself and your life as it pertains to your clients. Say you are selling belt buckles: you can talk about how you wore a particular style buckle and what event you wore it to. Perhaps you are a chef. You could show your family enjoying one of the meals you put together.

This approach allows your audience to get to know you. Going this route is a personal choice, and it's not for everyone or every venture. Many women entrepreneurs have used themselves and their families successfully to move their venture along and have had fun getting to know their audiences on a personal level as well.

Making this choice should be a carefully thought-out decision. Some women don't like to get personal, and that's okay too. But many times, by sharing your life and your family's life, buyers get to know you and feel more comfortable working with you and buying from you.

So get started. In this age of high connectedness, you want to stay in touch, and a newsletter is a great way to get to know your base of potential clients and to help them get to know you. Make sure your friends and family are on your list—they will be your first clients.

 IN YOUR NOTEBOOK

Record ideas for possible content and features for your e-letter. Be sure to add to this list as you gain experience with this format.

Assignment #5: Consider Flyers

Time to get the word out the old-fashioned way. Create a flyer to hand out, post in town, and put on message boards. I know this seems antiquated, but these do bring in clients if done properly.

Your flyer can be designed easily and inexpensively using many of today's word processing applications. But if graphic design is not your strong suit, find a friend or ask around for a contact who specializes in graphic design to help. (You can offer to barter for this service.)

To be an effective marketing tool, your venture's flyer should have three elements:

1. A compelling headline:
    "Get the Computer Help You Need"
    "Dog Walking When YOU Need it."
    "A home-cooked meal delivered to your doorstep."

2. A clear message: Concise descriptive list of the product or services you provide with your contact info and pricing.
3. A promotional offer:
   "Call before June 30th to receive 15% off on the first visit."
   "Call now for a free wardrobe assessment and consultation."
   "First hour is free to new clients."

Make sure the type is large and legible from a distance and includes your logo, venture name, description of your service or product, contact information, and a line or two about what you offer. For example, if you are offering a dog-walking service, you might say something like, "We know the best places in town that all the dogs love!" and include a photo of a dog. Dog lovers will look closer. Use tear-off tabs at the bottom with your phone number and email.

Put your flyer up at grocery stores, post offices, vet's offices, the entrances to dog parks, on the YMCA bulletin board, the church bulletin board—basically anywhere there's a corkboard for such postings.

Many people look at these when they are waiting in line, in the waiting room of doctors' offices, or talking with friends. Don't let the idea of a flyer get by you. One mom I know posted a flyer offering computer help on the store window of her dry cleaners. This attracted her first client, who then referred her to others.

Get creative with your flyers. One mom who was starting a cookie business stapled a wrapped cookie to a flyer and gave them out to everyone in her son's nursery school class. A mom who was starting a personalized Pilates venture handed out flyers to women leaving the grocery store. Think of creative ways to get your flyers into the hands of potential customers.

 IN YOUR NOTEBOOK

List ideas for content, layout, and placement for your flyers. Make notes of what gets results and what doesn't.

Assignment #6: Define Your Target Market

In this and the next four weeks you'll be marketing your venture. It's key to market to the right people. Who will buy your product or use your service? You could have the greatest cake pops in the world, but if you are only telling gluten-free eaters about them, you're not likely to get a sale. The following questions will help you identify the market for your venture.

* Who will buy your product?
* Where do they live?
* How old are they?
* Do they have kids?
* How old are their kids?
* What places of business do they frequent?

The answers to all of these questions will help you in placing your efforts in areas where your target market can find you. Let's say you have a consulting business that helps parents get their babies to sleep. Your target audience is new moms, likely with one or more children, newborn through age five. They live in the suburbs and go to the parks and nursery schools in town. They probably shop at the local baby store and frequent the local sandwich shop that caters to kids. This makes sense since your venture is local. If you have a service or product that can be provided beyond the local area, your reach can be beyond the local area.

Define who your target market is and concentrate your efforts with that group.

 IN YOUR NOTEBOOK

Make a list of all the groups that could be part of the target market for your product or service. This could include friends and family, past and present school contacts (yours and your childrens'), local retailers, professional and civic associations—any person or group that's likely to be interested in what you're offering. Update this list as you gain experience promoting your venture.

Reaching your target audience through email and other technologies today can be done so easily. That's the goal for this week.

TELLING THE WORLD SUCCESS STORIES

As you learned in Assignment #6, determining your target market is a vital part of your journey to success. Read about how the following moms found their markets and kick-started their business.

RT Picture Works: Bambi Riegel and Gwynne Tibbetts

Bambi and Gwynne started a video production service venture and knew their best customers would be their local friends. To announce their new business, they drafted an email and sent it out to everyone in their contacts list. Their friends told their friends and so on. They had a client base from one email.

Who knew a walk with a friend would turn into a business? Gwynne Tibbetts had come from a film production background and had a list of varied and interesting projects to her credit. Freelancing when she had children, Gwynne eventually stopped working to focus on family.

Bambi Riegel had a career in finance up until 2001, but with four kids, she turned to coaching girls' sports at a private school. Always an avid photographer, Bambi began to photograph sporting events and produce highlight videos for athletes. "But I always knew I wanted to make it a business," she says.

Gwynne wanted to get back into production of some kind, and a friend said, "You have to talk with Bambi." The two met and took a walk, and realized then and there they were going to work together. "We decided to produce videos—covering requests for everything from corporate videos to birthdays, anniversaries, graduations, sports banquets, and rehearsal dinners." Through word of mouth, they got their first assignment. They had fun creating the video, and the client loved the result. They were off and running. So they formed an LLC. (An LLC is particularly recommended when you are forming a partnership. It's a legal entity that can be set up by consulting an attorney or by going to one of the many websites offering legal services.)

A recent video production for a 50th birthday party is a good example of how these moms work. They gathered photographs, film, and music, and recorded and edited interviews with friends and family. The finished product was an emotional and poignant look at the birthday girl's life. "We look at someone's life like chapters in a book and work to showcase each important aspect, while making each video unique and personal." It usually takes a month or two to collect everything they'll need, but it all comes together in a 15- to 20-minute video. The finished product speaks to the time they spend on each project.

Gwynne and Bambi also photograph client events and post the images on their website for the client to view and order. Their observation that "In the current age, video really tells the story" explains one reason why this venture was the right idea at the right time. Bambi and Gwynne also had a very good understanding of their target market—women like themselves, in their 30s to 50s, with children, living in their area—basically, their friends and their friends' friends. Just one email to both their lists, telling everybody they knew about their new business, and they were off and running.

They look forward to expanding this fun—and thriving—business to do more work for corporations, charity events, and schools.

TAKEAWAY

- Your target market could be your family and friends, as it was for Bambi and Gwynne.
- Sometimes what you offer is something that you'd like or could use yourself, and so would your friends and their friends. If this is the case, start your marketing efforts with your circle of friends.

Back to Basics Wellness: Kathy D'Agati and Ellen Harnett

Kathy and Ellen started their venture offering one-on-one nutritional counseling, but they soon realized they wanted to reach a broader audience. They set up their nutritional program in the form of a daily email and now sell packages where members get this regular email with information and tips as they go through the recommended nutritional transformation. Each email has a suggested change for lifestyle and diet. These two grandmothers figured out the delivery system themselves and so can you.

What happens when two grandmothers set their minds to making a significant change? This is what Kathy D'Agati and Ellen Harnett did. When Kathy D'Agati's son was diagnosed with cancer, she went to work learning everything she could about nutrition. Her plan was to nourish him back to health.

Ellen Harnett's plan was to promote healthy eating with her own reci-pes, developed as a self-trained natural food chef. When her mom was diagnosed with cancer and the chemotherapy affected her taste for food, Ellen went to work developing recipes that were both nutritious and ap-pealing. A sufferer of acid reflux and IBS herself, Ellen had worked to create a healthy "gut-friendly" diet that had resulted in a significant im-provement in her condition.

Then these two friends took an intensive program at the Institute for Integrative Nutrition in New York City, which provides an online nutri-tional counseling degree. It was a year-long program followed by an "im-mersion program" that was taught by some of the best-known nutrition experts in the country. At this point the two women saw that they shared the same passion and goals and decided to start a business together. They would create a program that would bring clients back to wellness through a process of coaching and instruction. They named their new venture Back to Basics Wellness.

"Our target market is women who are forty-five to sixty years old and coming into their own. These women realize they can't eat what they used to and many are suffering from weight gain, headaches, joint pain, sleep issues, and exhaustion," say Kathy and Ellen. They believe that gluten, dairy, and sugar are among the culprits contributing to many of these symptoms. "Our goal is to make it simple for busy women to prepare de-licious meals that take away hunger and eliminate cravings so they can have sustainable weight loss and all-day energy."

They started by telling their own friends and building a list of email recipients. Each week, they sent out a letter with recipes and suggestions for healthy living. They were offering free information but also introducing their followers to their one-on-one programs, for which they charge a fee. This inexpensive strategy allowed them to get their first clients and build their reputation locally. And while months of study and preparation pre-ceded the launch of their business, the actual setup and delivery of their first mailing was done in a very short time.

As they garnered participants in the one-on-one nutritional programs, the two women realized they could reach more people if they created a virtual program that anyone with access to a computer could follow. They developed a paid subscription e-letter service. Clients can sign up for the program and receive updates via email. Every day a participant receives a newsletter through the email service with information and suggestions for the day. The daily tip might be to drink eight glasses of water, or to eliminate sugar—all part of the healthy eating program the two women advocate. Subscribers also get a list of foods to choose from and recipes to create from the suggested foods. The rewards are ongoing: "So many of our clients tell us we have changed their lives through food, and that is extremely satisfying."

"Creating our own website," Ellen says, "was a slow and painful process, but we did it." A friend helped them set up a shopping cart and incorporate it into the new site. Their email lists continued to grow. These were kept on an email marketing service so that they could easily send updates on programs and public appearances. They were also able to cue up daily letters to participants in advance.

These are two grandmothers on a mission; they are passionate about their message and driven to be heard. Kathy and Ellen have corporate clients as well, which, as they point out, "allows us to reach a larger audience at one time and keep our prices affordable." This business, which began with a weekly email, has continued to grow and prosper.

TAKEAWAY

- Kathy and Ellen knew their target market to be women in their 40s and 50s looking to eat more healthfully, so they collected email addresses from this target group.
- Their free newsletter offers recipes and healthy eating tips and promotes their paid programs. If this strategy would work for your venture, consider starting a free newsletter.

Easel Does It: Meredith Hubbard and Tracy Gohl

Meredith and Tracy wanted to start an in-home art class, and their target audience was all the moms they knew in their hometown. What better way than an email to advertise a new service? It's free, easy, and immediate. That's what they did and their venture was launched.

What kind of venture can you create that lets you bring your kids with you, needs little start-up cash, and makes money from day one? That's what neighbors and new friends Meredith Hubbard and Tracy Gohl asked each other when the economic crisis put their families in need of extra income. When they found themselves together at a play date, each with two kids under six years old, discussing budget cuts in the creative curriculum at their schools, they came up with an idea.

Having backgrounds in event planning and teaching preschool, arts, and theatre, both moms loved the idea of an arts and crafts class. They were on the same page about a class that would allow preschool children a more unstructured environment to explore their creativity. The key feature was that siblings of a broad age range would be able to attend. So rather than have mom run all over town dropping one child at one location and another somewhere else, they envisioned a class that catered to siblings. And better yet, they could bring the class to you.

Meredith and Tracy thought about their own needs as mothers and created the workshop around what they would want if they were enrolling their children. They decided to offer a 45-minute class that would come to where the mothers needed them. Calling their new venture Easel Does It, and with the tag line, "We bring all the fun, and take all the mess," the moms were ready to get started.

Initially offering in-home classes—theirs or yours—they got the word out with flyers at local preschools, told all their friends with kids in the target age group, and emailed everyone they knew around their hometown of Huntington Beach, California. Starting with preschool-level classes, Meredith and Tracy brought their younger kids with them—no babysitter needed. As word of mouth grew their business, Meredith and Tracy looked at other possibilities. They reached out to the local Parks and Recreation department by submitting a proposal and were hired to offer their class two days a week. This was the start of a more full-time commitment. From there they branched out to Parks and Recreation departments in neighboring towns. Now these two moms have their dream job: four to five days a week, two to three classes a day, in three towns.

Keeping true to their original plan for the business, Easel Does It allows the child to choose from a large selection of projects and provides "art stations" so kids can move from craft to craft. The projects range from beading to finger painting to paper collages and use all kinds of items like rocks, wooden spoons, and shoeboxes. Meredith and Tracy have added customized projects for birthdays to their schedule, catering to the child's areas of interest or theme of the party.

So with virtually no start-up costs, Meredith and Tracy were able to build a career that fit their needs. Tracy says, "I love that we have been able to create our own schedules around the thing that is most important to us—our kids and families."

Looking to the future, these partners are expanding and hiring teachers—more moms who want this kind of flexibility. Summer camps are on the docket, and they're thinking of a storefront. With no business plan, not even something written on a napkin, Meredith and Tracy started with one mobile art class and grew from there.

TAKEAWAY

- Tracy and Meredith saw a need that they could fill, developed a solution, and made it into a business.
- One email sent to all of their friends who were in the same situation (needing creative activities for siblings) and Easel Does It had its first paying class.
- They expanded their business by looking at other possible uses for their service. Look at how you can expand your venture by considering different uses for your offerings.

———

Next week you'll look at whether to blog or not.

nine

Week 9:
Join the Blogosphere

She was looking for an outlet where she could share a recipe, a great book, or a find from a shopping expedition, so Ridgely Brody started a blog. Calling it Ridgely's Radar, her blog allows friends and family to hear about a book she recently read, get her recipe for caramelized onion dip, or buy the rain boots she loves. By reaching out through social media Ridgely got more than friends and family to follow her. With no plan in mind, she just started sharing. And she says by starting a blog she learned how blogging can help a business grow.

Ridgely runs her own public relations firm and shares her blogging experience with her clients. To monetize her blog, she became an affiliate marketer with several groups so that when she recommends a cheese grater from William Sonoma or a favorite book that can be found on Amazon, followers can click through and buy the item. Through her affiliate marketing relationships, Ridgely gets a small percentage from each item sold for helping to promote the products and books. She then keeps the items listed in her online store so followers can easily shop for all of her favorite picks. Posting every Monday, Wednesday, and Friday, she's hooked. "Whether I write about transitioning your closet or a new wreath for Halloween, I get a real kick out of it." She says it's especially gratifying when someone tells her that her advice on a book, product, or recipe was spot on.

A blog can be your whole venture or it can be a marketing tool. Some bloggers share their views and experiences so successfully that they become recognized in their field. Like Stacey Bewkes, who founded the *Quintessence Blog*. She posted for over a year before her expertise was noticed in the design arena. From that recognition she has developed a speaking career and been a featured guest at many events in the design world. See Stacey's story later in this chapter.

This week is not about starting a blog but rather considering what a blog can do for you. You need to determine whether a blog makes sense for your venture now or down the road.

WEEK 9 ASSIGNMENTS

This week's assignments are designed to help you understand what goes into creating a blog and decide if it would make sense for you. This week you'll identify blogs you like and develop some content to use should you decide to start a blog.

Assignment #1: Find and Follow Blogs You Like

Identify people in your field of interest and follow their blogs. What do you like about their content? Are they selling a product or providing a service? Does their post make you want to buy it? Does their blog help you get to know them? Does it make you laugh, cry, think? Does the blog educate or provide insight? Follow some bloggers who write about things you like but who are not necessarily in the same area as your venture. Ask yourself why the blog exists. Is the author seeking to sell something, to express an opinion, or to garner a reputation as an expert? Keep notes in your Notebook.

Some bloggers want to demonstrate their expertise in their field in the hope of being offered a paying job. Take Amy Currie, who for several years ran her blog, *Secrets of a Home Cook*. Amy just recently was offered a paying job with an online news site. Although she didn't set out to get a job with her blog, the expertise she displayed there led to this opportunity.

Crafting a good plan for a blog requires a great deal of thought. Which is why this week, it's all about following and learning. Understanding the purpose of various blogs will help you consider if blogging is right for you.

IN YOUR NOTEBOOK

Make a list of the blogs you enjoy reading—whatever the topic. For each one, record what features you like and what's appealing about them. What's the purpose of the blog? Does the writer achieve it?

Assignment #2: Make a List of What You'd Blog About

Once you start to follow bloggers that you like and bloggers in your field, you'll get a sense of what they talk about. Should you decide to start a blog, you'll want your blog posts to be engaging—not a sales pitch for your product or service. A good example of how a blog can sell without trying is when a blogger provides content about an issue and then says, "By the way, my product or service can help you with this issue."

You don't have to be a writer to provide useful information and ultimately promote your product or service. Think about what your reader is interested in and either write your own content or provide a link to someone else's content. Many blogs simply direct their followers to other articles that are relevant. Content you prepare for your e-letter can be posted on your blog as well. Some followers prefer to get your information via an e-letter, while others prefer a blog format. You could have followers on both lists.

What's in a blog post? Blogging is a subtle sales technique. Say you're selling custom pillows. You could talk about the material you used for the pillows and show the pillows on a couch in a different room with each post. In this example you are not overtly saying, "Use me to create custom pillows for you," but rather saying, "Look how cool these pillows look in different settings." It's a soft sell, where you talk about a general topic and show how using your product or service follows naturally.

Another approach to crafting a blog post involves telling a story about how your product helped someone—for example, when a baby item solves a problem that a new mother is facing. Let's say you've created a unique sleeper that helps a newborn sleep through the night. You could tell readers how a mom who was up countless times each night with a newborn discovered your sleeper, and found that it helped her baby sleep longer.

Or if your product is a dog harness to help owners walk large dogs, you could include a picture of a dog and his owner and tell their story. Stories of users provide a great opportunity to showcase how your product helps clients. Each new client can provide another blog post.

You can use the same kinds of stories to showcase a service. Let's say you're providing a meal service for families. You could talk about the client who is a working mom. Describe how she needs a meal on the table every night when she gets home and how happy she is to find a prepared meal in the refrigerator waiting to be reheated. You could post about what you provided for dinner each night and show a photo of the meal.

Be careful not to use personal names or photos unless you get permission. You can also just use a description, such as, "One working mom using my food service says my garlic chicken is the best, and her kids ask for it every week." Stories make great testimonials and can be the basis of many interesting blog posts.

 IN YOUR NOTEBOOK

Start a list of ideas for your blog posts, including customer stories and testimonials.

Assignment #3: Develop a Short Posting Plan

Here are some suggestions for what you could post and when. Some bloggers post every day, some once a week, some once a month. And some post when they feel like it. Followers like consistency, so, should you decide to start a blog, I suggest setting a schedule and following it as best you can.

Product Post Ideas

For a fashion item, show a complete outfit that incorporates something from your line. This idea is great for scarves, necklaces, bracelets, belts, tunics, sweaters—basically any fashion item that you can build an outfit around. Put together a collage of the items you would wear with your product. You can either do this using PowerPoint and choosing items from the universe of clothes on the Web, or you can use your own clothes. Maybe you use jeans and a white T-shirt to showcase a different scarf with each blog post. Or a little black dress to showcase your line of necklaces. Wrap these ideas around a schedule.

Here's a possible posting schedule for a line of scarves:

Monday: How I wore it (show a photo of you wearing a scarf).

Wednesday: How they wore it (show a photo of a celebrity wearing a scarf).

Friday: Featured scarf (show a closeup of a scarf from your line with a link to purchase).

Service Post Ideas

If you run a dog-walking venture, tell a story about a walk with one of your charges; or blog about the weather for the upcoming weekend, or about a new place to walk, or about a dog park you recently visited. If you offer an exercise class, blog about nutritional tips. If you provide home organization, show before and after photos of projects. If you are involved with a charity, show an event where you donated your service.

Here's a possible schedule for a nutritionist blog:

Monday: Snack food idea (post a photo of a healthy snack).

Wednesday: Showcase a healthy lifestyle tip.

Friday: Post a recipe for a healthy dinner entrée.

Food Item Post Ideas

Post recipes, healthy ways to cook various items, meal plans, or how to serve your item. How about blogging about various dishes that you find in other blogs you follow? Or you could blog about a dish you had at a local restaurant and how your food item would complement it.

Possible blogging schedule for a granola vendor:

Monday: A customer of the week enjoying your granola.

Wednesday: Feature a new shop or market that carries your granola.

Friday: A different exercise you did before enjoying your granola—a hike, a yoga class, a spin class, a rock-climbing session, walking your dog. (This post provides great opportunities to include a photo.)

It could take some time to decide what your strategy will be, but try to come up with something this week. Remember, you may not implement it if you decide it's not right for you right now. And you may use it later. But it's important to go through the exercise so you can decide if blogging makes sense for your venture. It will also help you gather information on your competitors' products or services to see how they differentiate themselves.

Many bloggers adopt an overall theme for their posts and don't assign specific names for their entries; rather, the post is identified by their brand. Followers get used to seeing the post come to their email box on the same day each week or at the same time each day.

Your plan may be to post only when you have an idea you want to share. But the most effective way to generate followers—and sales—is to be consistent. Should you decide to start blogging, you can set up a link on your website that allows followers to sign up to have your blog posts delivered to their inbox.

 IN YOUR NOTEBOOK

Collect ideas for a possible blog posting plan and schedule for your product or service.

Assignment #4: Write Some Trial Blog Posts

Writing a few blog posts is a great exercise. It will help you figure out what topics you'd blog about and how you'd present them. It will also help you develop your blogging voice. And you'll get a sense of the time commitment involved. Blog posts should be short and concise, usually between 200 and 500 words in length.

Many of the blog hosting services allow you to set the time and date for your post to go live. That way, if you know you're going to be away or too busy to write, you can set up a month's worth of posts in one sitting and they will post automatically throughout the month. So whatever is going on in your life, your blog will continue. This can be extremely helpful.

Assignment #5: Decide Whether a Blog Makes Sense

Blogging may not be a productive activity for your venture at this point. This is why this week's assignment is to consider blogging rather than to start a blog. A blog is quite a commitment. However, if you want to be recognized in your field, I feel that blogging is imperative. Take, for example, Pam Pik's college counseling business. Pam's blog was the perfect extension to her website. It assisted her in marketing her venture. But it was something that came later.

So while it would be great to get a blog up and running, your assignments this week are designed to help you consider whether blogging is the right tool for you, right now. Keep the information you gather in your Notebook for when you feel it's time to add a blog to your venture. You'll know when.

 ## IN YOUR NOTEBOOK

Make a list of pros and cons for starting a blog for your venture.

Assignment #6: Starting a Blog (optional)

If your venture is to start a blog, here's your to-do list.

Step 1: Pick a Host
The following are several hosts that I like:

- www.blogger.com
- www.wordpress.com
- www.createblog.com
- www.squarespace.com/tour/bloggers
- www.thoughts.com

Each of these hosts will make it easy to get started with your blog. Peruse each and choose one. You'll want to use your name, logo, and colors to brand your blog. You can do this yourself or get some help to make your "skin" (the look of the blog) showcase your brand.

Step 2: Come Up with Your Posting Plan
Look at what others do and get creative. Tailor your plan to fit your message, your audience, and your schedule.

Step 3: Write and Publish One Post
If you want to start a blog, most likely you know what you want to talk about. Check your Notebook for ideas and inspiration and just get started. You'll learn as you go.

Entire books, articles, and, yes, blog posts have been written on the subject of blogging. My purpose here is to get you started so you can grow and learn as you go. Do one post and keep going.

Step 4: Monetize your blog

Many people ask how you make money with a blog. The most common way is through advertising or product placement. A company pays you to talk about their product or include an ad or promo on your blog. Affiliate marketing can create another income stream like the example at the start of the chapter, Ridgely's Radar. Here's how affiliate marketing works: You sign up to be an affiliate of Amazon. Then you write and post about a book or product from Amazon with a link to buy that item. Amazon gives you an affiliate code to use. When someone clicks through and buys that item with your code you'll get a percentage of the sale.

There are affiliate marketing groups that represent a number of different stores and e-commerce sites. You'd look to what your interests are to see if there was a fit. For example, let's say you start a fitness blog and love the new recipe book by a fitness guru. You'd blog about it and set up a click-through to buy using your affiliate code from Amazon. Or let's say you blog about a fitness bracelet that is offered by a particular online shop. You'll find a link to become an affiliate of that shop on their site. Click through and sign up. Many times you'll be directed to an affiliate group that they are part of. So you'll not only become an affiliate of that shop but others too. You can peruse them to see what you'd like to promote. At the bottom of e-commerce sites you'll generally see a link for affiliates that will give you the details of that site's arrangement with affiliates.

Some people blog to promote themselves as experts in their field, which can lead to book deals, speaking engagements, and writing assignments. The most common way to create income through a blog is to lead people to your product or service through your blog.

BLOGGING SUCCESS STORIES

Whether a blog is your venture itself or you use a blog to promote your venture, you should have an understanding of how a blog works to build your business. See how these women use their blogs, and make a decision if it's right for you.

Quintessence Blog: Stacey Bewkes

Stacey Bewkes is an avid reader of everything from the New York Times *to* Italian Vogue. *She can't find enough time in her day for all the interesting articles she looks to devour. And then what to do with this abundance of information? With a strong need to express herself, this mom decided to start a blog.*

"I'm one of those people who has a wealth of information on a lot of things but no one to share it with. A blog seemed perfect for me." Stacey Bewkes didn't have the younger generation's tech savvy, so she taught herself how to use WordPress and add photos and then she began to put her musings on the Web.

Her blog became her passion even if no one was reading it. "I loved creating an article on something I found interesting. It was like I was writing for a magazine that I had created." Stacey gave herself the task of posting every day during the week. She named her blog Quintessence.

She wrote about everything from a jewelry auction at Christie's to her favorite old movies. Stacey loves to learn about architecture, art, jewelry, clothing, and design; she then shares her findings and thoughts in her blog posts.

Stacey had no idea where her blog would take her or if anyone was reading it. But her interesting stories got noticed on the Web, and in a short time (about six months) she built an audience. When people would search for a particular item that interested them, Stacey's post would come up. They would follow her and tell other friends to do the same. This is how her audience grew.

With 17 years as an art director at Simon and Schuster, Stacey left work after her third child was born. It was years later, when her youngest child was 10, that she started blogging and got hooked. "It's all I want to do." Her husband was baffled: "So what are you going to do with this?" Stacey didn't know at the beginning, but she knew she had to keep posting.

So where did her blog take her? When her blog was noticed by people in the fashion and design world, Stacey was recruited to be an inaugural member of the Blog Tour Team at the London Design Festival. This was a great place to network and promote her blog. She was then asked to speak at select design venues such as Fashion Group International's regional director's conference at Condé Nast, AmericasMart in Atlanta, and the D&D Building in New York City.

Who knew writing about things that she found interesting would lead to this? Stacey's success has been extraordinary. *Quintessence* has been featured in numerous publications, and has won a number of awards, including the 2013 Design Bloggers Hall of Fame for best blog and the 2012 American Home Furnishings Alliance (AHFA) HOME Award for outstanding journalism in the new category of social media.

Stacey built her reputation as a writer through her blog and has had job offers with several publications, but for now she's having too much fun attending events as a featured guest. Her video series with Susanna Salk is getting traction as well.

"Getting validation shows me that readers are enjoying what I have to say. I'd love to write for some other upscale publications or perhaps have an online magazine some day." Who knows? Look how far she's gotten by putting her thoughts together in a creative way and posting them.

TAKEAWAY

- Stacey was not sure where her blog would take her, but she loved doing it and followed her passion.
- As her audience grew, her reputation grew, and people in the design world reached out to her.
- Stacey has found a niche and built a strong social media presence.

Secrets of a Home Cook: Amy Currie

After publishing two cookbooks, Amy Currie wanted to share with a larger online audience, so she started a blog. A blog helped her to gain recognition in her field. And her blog allowed her to reach a wider audience, which led to speaking engagements and some paying jobs as a writer.

How do you turn a simple task into a venture? That's what Amy Currie asked herself about preparing meals for her family. She began her career selling advertising for magazines but when her twins came along, "Racing home to get there so the nanny could leave just wasn't working."

Amy had always loved to cook and learned the basics sitting at her Philadelphia grandmother's kitchen table. "After leaving the workforce, I knew I wanted to start something I could do from home." So when a friend asked her to cater a party, she agreed. Other business soon followed, and Amy developed a niche for her catering business. She specialized in foods "before and after": "Hostesses would do the main course and ask me to do appetizers before the meal and provide dessert for after the meal."

Her catering business grew, but Amy's heart was really in preparing meals for her family. "I wanted to share the recipes I used myself with other moms. I found that celebrity chef recipes don't always translate to what you'd make for your family." She had found ways to put together a great meal in 10 minutes, something every mom needs.

When her kids were settled into elementary school, Amy says, "I went on a mission to reevaluate my life." Amy's creative outlet became gathering the recipes she used, and recipes from her family and husband's family, into a cookbook. When the time came to publish these recipes, she found it more prudent to self-publish. "It took six months once I had the content. I was the writer, editor, designer, and producer. I knew it was a hit, because I became the 'Dear Abby' of recipe advice. I discovered I was quite good at doling out tips and helpful hints to home cooks." So she promptly published another book. This led to teaching at a local cooking school and writing assignments for a range of publications.

This was when Amy turned to blogging. "I wanted to share with a larger audience and I realized I could take what I had done in my books and build a platform with a blog." She began adding demonstrations in the form of how-to videos once a week on her blog, *Secrets of a Home Cook*, and on a network of New Jersey online news sites. "I was even asked to audition for the Food Network show *Chopped*."

Amy has focused her goal on becoming the next Rachel Ray or Ina Garten. "I'm setting my goals high to see how far I can get. I know I have a need to cook and publish to be fulfilled. Blogging allows me to share my journey in the kitchen and beyond." Amy's intent on educating herself on social media. She uses Facebook, Twitter, Pinterest, Instagram, and her blog to build her following and her brand. Part of her learning process is studying what others in her professional space have done and figuring out what has led to their success. With energy, enthusiasm, and dedication, she hopes to turn her cooking and blogging into a sustainable success.

TAKEAWAY

- Building on her experience as a self-published author, Amy began a blog to build an online platform and expand her audience. Think about whether doing the same would help to grow your venture.

Fairfieldista Blog: Ann Quasarano

Ann Quasarano was writing for two local blogs when she realized she could use her columns to start her own blog. Her long-term goal is to get a position with a large news service, but she knew she had to prove herself and build an audience. Starting her own blog allowed her to do just that.

Freelancing can lead to your own venture. That's what happened with Ann Quasarano when she was writing two columns for a news website that covered happenings in her local community. Ann had worked for Warner Brothers before her son was born, organizing premier parties and reaching out to the press for these huge events. "I did a lot of red-carpet movie premiers including some of the Harry Potter movies. It was really fun but high stress and lots of pressure." After her son was born, she decided to step away from the spotlight to stay home with her baby.

"I did some PR for local businesses, and as my son got older, I found I had more time to build my client base." Ann also got a job writing for a local news website. She covered people and businesses from her hometown each week and was paid for her writing. But when the blog shifted to a different business model and could no longer pay freelancers, Ann decided to go out on her own. "I thought, why not start my own blog about Fairfield County and continue to add to my reputation as a writer?" Ann's ultimate goal is to be hired to write for a large blog, website, or magazine by the time her son is in high school.

Working with a designer, someone she knew from her past career in Manhattan, she created her blog and named it *Fairfieldista*, combining the name of her county with a play on the term "fashionista." In the "About" section of her blog, Ann asks, "Who has time to drive up and down I–95 and the Post Road looking for the perfect outfit for the school fundraiser, locate that great (undiscovered) caterer, and scour every local newspaper/

website/magazine/Twitter and Facebook feed to find all the cool stuff that's happening in Fairfield County?" Ann bills her blog as the place to find everything you need to know about what's happening in her area. Her blog page allows the reader to search by their own town and by fashion, food, family, or fun.

Ann finds that having her own blog gives her the flexibility she wants in her life while her son is young. She says, "I don't want to wait to build my resumé until after he goes to college. Doing my blog is helping me get started early." This way she'll have real experience when she goes out to get a job with another company in a few years. Amy uses social media to put out a CTA, or call to action, for readers and followers to sign up for her blog. She says, "I always have a call to action in anything I publish so readers know what I'm asking for."

What is a CTA? A CTA asks the readers to take a particular action. Whether you want your readers to comment, sign up for your newsletter, or Like your Facebook page, it's key to ask them to engage.

"I love the challenge of finding new and relevant stories to write about for my blog." Ann's husband and son think it's pretty cool too. She's been asked to post for *Fairfield County Moms Blog* and reblog for the *Connecticut Post*. Reblogging is when you post the same blog to an additional site. It seems her blogging venture has turned into her new paying job.

TAKEAWAY

- A blog can help you showcase your skills and build your resumé for getting hired by a firm. Consider if this makes sense for you. Remember that it's also possible to generate income from a blog.

———

Blogging can be your entire venture or a means to an end. Either way, there are options for you should you decide to start a blog as your venture or blog to promote your venture. Next week, you'll build your presence on social media.

ten

Week 10:
Do Some Social Media Networking

When Jayne Benson wanted to get the word out about her new venture, she turned to the Web and social networking sites. Her venture began when other moms at her children's school saw the cupcake creations she brought in for snack time, and Jayne realized she could create a business teaching others the art of the cupcake. She organized classes and cupcake-making parties to cover everything from batter to icing to making cupcake characters.

When it was time to spread the word about her cupcake-making parties, Jayne figured the easiest way to reach her target audience—local moms—would be through Facebook. She could post photos of her latest creations and let her friends know that she was offering her services: not only for planning and running kids' birthday parties or after-school activities, but also for ladies' nights. Using Facebook was the fastest way to get the word out and tell everyone she knew that she could bring the cupcake-making fun to them.

The whole world is using social media and so should you. It's easy once you get started; don't let the process intimidate you. Most moms with their own ventures weren't sure how to update their status on Facebook, tweet on Twitter, or pin to Pinterest when they got started, but after trying social media, they quickly got the hang of it, and you will too.

For many, social media remains a mystery, so I'm going to give you a few simple ideas to begin your social media education and campaign. You can take it so much further than what you'll find here when you're ready to do more. Get started with at least a few things and learn as you go. If you knew all that you could do, it would be overwhelming. Right now it's enough to get started.

WEEK 10 ASSIGNMENTS

This week you'll be creating a Facebook fan page, starting a Twitter account, and setting up your venture on Pinterest. On each of the platforms you'll begin to build followers this week. You'll also draft an initial social media posting plan. This is a busy week, so let's get started.

Assignment #1: Create a Facebook Fan Page

You must do this through your own personal Facebook page, so if you don't have a personal page yet, start there. Sign up for a personal Facebook page at www.facebook.com. If you already have a personal page, visit www.facebook.com/pages to start your fan page (business page). There is a link at the bottom of the left-hand column on your personal page to create a new page. This takes you to some choices: Are you a local business or place, a company, organization, or institution, a brand or product, etc.?

Most likely your venture can be classified as a local business or place, or a brand or product. Then you'll be asked to choose your category from a drop-down menu. If you can't find an exact fit, get as close as possible.

You must set up the fan page from your personal page. If you're not a Facebook person, no worries, you can provide minimal information on your personal page. Your fan page, however, should be customized with your logo, photo, tag line, and other information about your product or service. Facebook will walk you through the simple steps to get started. If you have trouble, reach out to a friend or contact with social media skills. Your Facebook fan page is the perfect vehicle to tell people about your new venture.

Assignment #2: Update Your Status

On your fan page, under "Status," you'll post information about your venture. Your first status update could be an introduction to your new service or product. Add several additional updates so that when a client pulls you up on Facebook, they see an active page filled with lots of posts.

Each post should be short and to the point, under 50 words. You can post a link to a longer article or something from your website if you choose. To post, write something and then add a photo using the icon of a camera below the box. Include photos with each post; followers like the visual aspect of following you. You can also schedule your post to be published at a later time. So if you want to post three times in a week but want to prepare all of your posts on Monday, Facebook allows you to do that using the clock icon below the Status box.

Here are some ideas for what to post. Let's say you are starting a dog-walking service. You could post some pictures of dogs or photos of places where you walk. "Took Spot to the park today. Great weather," and include a photo of Spot in the park. If you create handcrafted paper products, post a photo of your latest design and write about your inspiration. "This card was inspired by the clouds I saw on my hike." For a computer-assistance service venture, post a task you helped someone complete along with a relevant photo. "Helped a client set up his new printer today," with a photo of a printer. Whatever your product or service, get creative. This can be so much fun.

Start to post the same kind of content or the same content you include in your newsletter— informative tips and suggestions related to your expertise or venture. Look at the ideas you came up with for a potential blog last week. These can be used on Facebook.

 IN YOUR NOTEBOOK

Keep a running list of ideas to use for Facebook posts, along with possible photos to post with them.

Assignment #3: Get Likes

The number of "Likes" that you have is the number of Facebook followers that you have, so you want to get as many as possible. These are the people who are seeing your posts. (Not everyone who Likes you sees every post. You may have to "boost" a post, and there is a cost for this.)

There are three ways to get Likes when logged into your fan page. While on your page, select "Build Audience" at the top of the page. This drop-down menu gives you three options:

1. Invite Email Contacts (you can import up to 5,000 contacts);
2. Invite Friends (you can send an invite to your Facebook friends asking them to Like your fan page); and
3. Share Page (on your own personal Facebook page, on a friend's timeline, in a group, or on a fan page you manage).

In addition to these three tools inside Facebook there are other ways to get more Facebook Likes. Ask your friends and family to Like you. If you have a regular newsletter, tell your newsletter subscribers about your page as well. Make sure you post your newsletter info on Facebook. Some users prefer to get their updates via Facebook rather than a weekly email letter.

Have a Facebook button in your email signature and at the bottom of your newsletter and on your website. This is optional, as it may take some technical skill to set up. Even if you don't add a button, be sure to include all your social media accounts in your email signature—for example, "Visit our website/Read our blog/Follow us on Twitter/Fan us on Facebook."

Offer special deals to users who Like you. "Like us on Facebook and your dog will get an extra 30 minutes with his first walk." "Post a comment and get a free doggie scarf with your first walk."

Engage your followers. Ask questions. You can do this in the status section. For example, "Where does your dog like to walk?" "Post a photo of your dog in his favorite collar." "Share a story about your dog." Your goal is to get your followers involved with you and with other followers on your page.

This gives you the basics to setting up on Facebook. Get started and you can build as you go.

Assignment #4: Open a Twitter Account

Next, open a Twitter account at www.twitter.com. Twitter accounts are set up under your company name. For example, VentureMom.com's Twitter account is @venturemom (this is called your Twitter "handle"). All Twitter accounts are preceded by the at sign, @. Make sure you use your company name and not own your name, unless they're the same. That way when clients search for your company on Twitter they will find your company rather than you. You can have an additional Twitter account for personal use.

Your company Twitter account should only be for business information—nothing personal. So if you are a dog walker and your company name is *For the Dogs*, your Twitter account would be @forthedogs. If this is already taken, try @4thedogs, or @4thedogsNY (or CT, or NH, etc.). Your Twitter handle is limited to 15 characters.

Assignment #5: Tweet

Post a tweet. When tweeting you want to provide short, useful suggestions related to your venture. You can use only 140 characters for each tweet. For a dog-walking service you might suggest a great path that you took your charges on: "Took Spot and Buster to Waveny Park today, trails were muddy so stayed on the roads, @forthedogs." Or "@forthedogs offering half-price walks on Mondays, email us for details." Or "To read a great article on keeping dogs cool in the summer, go to _____." Insert the Web address where the article can be found.

Tweets will come up in your followers' feed. If your followers also follow hundreds of other people, your tweet may get lost, so post often. Post the same tweet multiple times. If you want to tell your followers about half-price Mondays, you could post that tweet four times a day. If your tweet is more specific, like the current weather on the walking trails, that could be posted every two hours on the same day after your outing with your dogs.

Assignment #6: Gather Twitter Followers

With Twitter, follow those who share the same interests. For example, if you offer a baby product, follow "mom" Twitter handles. (Go to twitter.com/search and enter mom in the Search bar. You'll be amazed.) You can do a search for like-minded Twitter feeds to follow by using keywords in your search, for example, "belts" or "cupcakes"; not all the handles that come up will be relevant to you, but this is an easy way to find people interested in the same thing. Twitter will also prompt you with possibilities of like-minded handles to follow as well. It's common Twitter courtesy to follow someone who follows you. Set aside about 15 minutes a day to tweet and find others to follow.

There is an art to building a Twitter following, and you can get very creative with your tweets. Follow someone in your field and see what they tweet about and then make your own plan to gather followers and potential customers. Twitter is also great for connecting with the media: your local newspaper, a magazine, news program, etc. Follow bloggers on Twitter who are relevant to your venture too.

 IN YOUR NOTEBOOK

Keep track of Facebook and Twitter ideas that you see others using. And keep a list of items that you want to post and tweet about.

Assignment #7: Set Up Pinterest

Pinterest is a site for setting up photo boards and sharing with other pinners. Your Pinterest boards can garner followers as well so it's a way to stay connected visually with your followers. Let's say your venture is being a florist. Pinterest is a great place to post your creations. In fact, anything that you create can be documented on Pinterest. Your followers will want to see what you post. And you can allow others to post on your boards. Your account should be set up in your company's name. To sign up for a business page, visit www.pinterest.com.

You can set up different boards depending on what you want to pin and what you want others to pin on your boards. You are looking for engagement from your Pinterest followers. In the florist example, you could set up a board for your arrangements, one for your arrangements in your clients' houses, other florists' arrangements that you like, magazine clippings of flowers in homes—the ideas are endless.

When setting up boards and naming them, keep in mind search keywords. People go on Pinterest and search to find pins, so ask yourself, "If I were looking for a service/product like mine, what keywords would I type in to find it?" Then use these keywords to name your boards; this will ensure that people will see your pins when they search. For example, "Floral Arrangements," "Flowers at Home," "Flowers I Like," etc.

If you are a stylist of some kind, whether for clothes, homes, or book-cases, take photos of your work and pin them on Pinterest. If you are in travel, set up boards for each trip you take. Pinterest is like creating scrapbooks. Remember how much fun that used to be? This is the same thing, but others get to pin to your board as well.

I'll give you an example from my own business. VentureMom.com has multiple boards on Pinterest. There are boards for services, food and drink, fashion products, and so on. You can visit our Pinterest boards to see how it works. Once you start on Pinterest it's hard to stop.

Follow other Pinterest users that are relevant to your venture. Bloggers are great to follow too. Re-pin other people's pins on your boards and they will get notification, and then they tend to pin your pins. You can even create a group board to get more exposure. A group, or community, board is the same as a regular board except other people are allowed to pin. When creating a group board you add the people you want by email or their Pinterest name (you must be following them before you can add them). Again, this can get a bit complicated, but I want you to get started with one board. So, this week's assignment is to open your account and create one board and pin one photo.

Assignment #8: Prepare a Social Media Plan

You'll want a plan for what you'll be posting and when. This assignment may carry over to later weeks or after Week 12, but your outlets will be set up and ready to go. Your plan can take less than an hour a week to execute. You can sign up for HootSuite or one of the other social media posting services (see Resources at the back of this book) to help you post to all of your social media. A service like this gives you the capability to schedule posts in advance on all social media platforms.

When developing your plan, mix in a variety of posts. For example:

* Ask a question.
* Take a poll.
* Show an image of you working.
* Add a testimonial—then ask if anyone else has a story to share.
* Post a contest or giveaway.
* Post something humorous.

- Post something personal—maybe a picture of your family; you are your brand, so people like a peek into your life to connect with you.
- Post a special offer.

There are many more types of posts, but these are just some to get you going.

 IN YOUR NOTEBOOK

Keep a list of your social media accounts and ideas for posting, including photos. Draft a schedule for posting to your various accounts.

This is a lot of information to digest. Don't get overwhelmed; your assignments this week are to set up a Facebook fan Page, a Twitter account, and a Pinterest account and post to each one.

SOCIAL MEDIA SUCCESS STORIES

At the beginning of this chapter you saw how Jayne Benson built her business using Facebook. In the following stories, you'll read how three other venture moms put social media to work for their business ventures.

Within Reason Estate Sales: Kelly Daniel and Amy Reehl

When Kelly and Amy helped a friend stage a tag sale, they had so much fun that they developed a business around it. Both had experience dealing with furniture, fabric, and art, so the idea was a good fit. Referrals were a huge part of their growth in the beginning, but Facebook became the ideal way to promote their sales and showcase the items being offered.

The first time they met was when their girls, Hailey and Bailey, had a play date. Moms Kelly Daniel and Amy Reehl hit it off immediately and ended up talking for three hours. They talked about wanting to start a business of some kind and through their conversation realized they both loved tag sales, antiques, and finding treasures.

Amy grew up with a father who dragged her to garage and estate sales when she was young, and she had a knowledge of textiles through her job with Laura Ashley. Kelly's mother opened an art gallery when she was in college, and while she was living in London antiques were a part of Kelly's life. She spent many hours at the antique fairs and shops there.

Fast-forward to life raising kids and running their own tag sales. A friend knew they were "tag sale savvy" and asked Kelly and Amy to help her sell her things on eBay. But she had so much stuff to sell they decided to hold a tag sale for her. Amy and Kelly had so much fun that they knew right away this was their business. Word of mouth spread the news, and when people asked what they did, they said, "We'll do anything to help clean out a house—move furniture, clean things, stage rooms. Anything within reason." That became their name when Kelly and Amy formed their LLC: Within Reason Estate Sales.

Having set up a game plan for spreading the word and a business model, Amy and Kelly were profitable with their first sale in July 2011. The model was simple; they would get a percent of the overall income from the items sold at each sale. The marketing plan in the beginning stages of their business involved sending postcards to homeowners who were selling their homes, which garnered lots of assignments. They found the addresses on real estate sites, and then they looked up the names. They also let the real estate community know they were available for running estate sales.

Facebook was a natural addition to their plan because it allowed them to reach a wide audience, and they could post upcoming sales multiple times in the week preceding the event. To build followers, they asked their friends to follow them on Facebook and included their Facebook link on every email they sent out.

For even more promotion, they posted the items the sale was offering on their Facebook fan page. "We post photos of things from the sale—this gets people excited about coming." Facebook added to their reach and is a great way for this team to target their audience. And at each sale, they handed out postcards with their information. Tag sale attendees who might have never heard of them were their best audience.

When asked about the competition, they say, "There are one or two firms that do this, but we're out to be the go-to estate sale girls." They feel they price things very competitively and therefore sell more and make more for their clients. Kelly and Amy do their research and are well versed in what things should sell for—everything from an antique bureau to a set of Wedgewood china. Amy says, "It's really hard work but we laugh the whole time, and every sale is different."

With a two-week lead time in the best-case scenario, Kelly and Amy prepare for the sale by researching, pricing, and merchandising items so they show in the best light. Sales usually run for two days, on Friday and Saturday. Their husbands care for their kids—six between them— on Saturdays. Booked weeks out, Within Reason is gaining on the competition.

TAKEAWAY

- Facebook allowed Within Reason to easily remind their followers of upcoming sales at no cost. Do the same for your business if you have upcoming events.
- Use your Facebook fan page to share all things relevant to your venture.

Peter Beaton Studio: Darcy Creech

Darcy Creech started with one item and created a brand. When she wore her straw hat to an event and it garnered multiple compliments, Darcy realized she might be able to create a business. After doing her research, she started her line and grew from there. Social media has been instrumental in branding the Peter Beaton Studio. While it took her longer than 12 weeks to get where she is today, she went from that first idea to her first sale within a short time.

Darcy Creech, the owner of Peter Beaton Studio, lives life full out. As the label on her rain boots says, "Leave a trail worth following." And she does just that.

Darcy's life as an entrepreneur began the day she created a hat for herself that drew attention from dozens of women. From this, she saw a niche for a product and began the process of learning what she needed to know to manufacture the classic straw hats that would become her trademark. From that first hat, she went on to build a roster of accounts that included Henri Bendel, Neiman Marcus, Barney's, Nordstrom, and two First Ladies. Within four years she went from being an inexperienced businesswoman with a passion for hats to a seasoned—and successful—entrepreneur. "My whole philosophy was to specialize in something and specialize deep. That's the way to stand out in a crowd," Darcy suggests.

Darcy moved to Nantucket in 1995 with her son to find a permanent home for her family and her growing business. Since then, Peter Beaton Studio (the name comes from her two sons' names) has grown to provide a wide range of classic clothing in tune with Nantucket's iconic New England style—handbags made of the same straw as her signature hats, striped sailor shirts for infants, children, and adults, and her version of Wellington boots.

Facebook, it turns out, is the perfect platform for Darcy to promote the many sides of her business. Darcy advertises sales in her shop, posts information about things going on in Nantucket, and showcases a variety of philanthropic causes. She's very involved with the shopkeepers group in Nantucket and uses her Facebook fan page to spread the word about their events and activities.

Through Facebook, Darcy not only brings people to the island, but she also brings customers into her shop. By branding her fan page, posting often, and making connections with other local businesses, she's created a presence that is instantly recognizable.

And while Darcy's business has grown over time, her first sale—of a hat similar to the one that started it all—came just a little over 12 weeks after the idea for her business was born.

TAKEAWAY

- For Darcy, focusing on one item and then expanding her line was key to her success.
- Use social media as a key ingredient in building your brand, your followers, and your clients, as Darcy has done.
- Provide your followers with fun information about local events. This builds followers.

White Moth Jewelry: Tracey Heinemann

The "Open See" at Henri Bendel opened up a whole new world for Tracey Heinemann and her jewelry line. Getting there at 4:00 A.M. was worth it when she was chosen to sell at the store. From there she reached out to boutiques around the country. Tracey actively uses Twitter and Facebook to keep her fans in the loop.

Tracey Heinemann has strong feelings about creating her jewelry line: "When you absolutely love what you do, you know it's right for you." During her past career in marketing beverages, Tracey learned that the look and feel of the design and packaging is critical to the success of a product. She saw how a unique piece of jewelry paired with a white T-shirt and jeans could change the whole look of a simple outfit. "I loved styling my friends and found myself wanting to create jewelry to complete the look we were working to achieve."

After sourcing materials and developing her product line, she began to show her pieces at trunk shows and holiday boutiques to build her brand awareness and get her first sale. But it was pitching Henri Bendel that really opened her eyes. "They have what they call 'Open See,' where you present your line to their buyers for an in-store trunk show. I showed up at four in the morning—and was ninth in the line that eventually stretched down Fifth Avenue. It was amazing to see what everyone had to present, and I learned so much talking to the people who were there to pitch." In this process, vendors get 90 seconds to tell their story and show their wares.

To her surprise, Tracey's jewelry line was chosen. "They said, 'We love it, you're in,' and I couldn't believe it." This vote of confidence gave Tracey what she needed to move forward. Reaching out to local boutiques and home design stores was the first order of business. This involved taking her line on the road and visiting stores and shops in person, first in her local area and then elsewhere. Through this initial push, the popularity of her line grew. Now she's in stores all over the country.

For Tracey, staying in touch with her fans is critical, and one way she does this is through Twitter. Her posting plan is simple: post on all social networks about trunk shows, new products, sales, press—anything about her business. Using Facebook, Pinterest, and Twitter helps her keep her clients up to date on her, the business, and her jewelry.

With her brand name starting to build, Tracey is experiencing some growing pains and may consider part-time employees to meet the demand for her jewelry. Her two boys sometimes help with production by polishing and packaging. "I love teaching them about running a small business and think it's a great learning experience for them."

Tracey's inspiration comes from her travels, and she hopes to venture farther to source unique materials to use in her designs.

Tracey knows she's in the right business because she feels just as passionate about creating jewelry now as she did when she started. "I feel great when I see a woman wearing a piece I created."

TAKEAWAY

- If you love what you're doing, you're more likely to be successful and better able to renew your creative energy.
- Post on a regular basis on all social media platforms to build followers.
- New items, sales, and events can all be shared on Twitter.

Next week you'll do more than social networking; you'll meet people and attend meetings to reach your target audience.

eleven

Week 11:
Do Some Real-Life Networking

When she saw a new trend in an old business, she pounced. Caterina DiLorenzo has always had a passion for baking and was often asked to supply one of her cakes for friends' parties. But when she noticed that cake pops were gaining popularity, she gathered her supplies and began experimenting. She started with the classic flavors: vanilla, chocolate, red velvet, and carrot. When she shared them with her circle of family and friends, the pops were a hit. Now she needed some orders.

Caterina needed to get the word out about her cake pops and felt that face-to-face networking with her target audience was key. She joined several local groups for moms in her community: CT Moms, Moms of Lower Fairfield Country, and No Drama Mamas and Papas of Fairfield County. She was able to share her venture idea with her target audience at the meetings of these groups. She also supported these groups by advertising Cat's Cake Pops in their newsletters. With the demand for cake pops growing, Cat's story was featured by several local news services. The orders came in. Caterina turned to Facebook next to expand her following. By focusing on a trendy item, she was the baker who got the call. Cat's Cake Pops doesn't have a website, but by networking in person and with her presence on Facebook Caterina now gets orders from all over the country.

Are you ready to meet new people? Clients are everywhere. Networking through groups that are made up of your target audience can be fun and interesting. These groups allow you to make all kinds of new contacts and friends and find clients and customers.

WEEK 11 ASSIGNMENTS

It's time to take it to the streets. Whether you meet people in line renewing your driver's license or chat with the women in your exercise class, get ready to network.

Assignment #1: Develop Your Elevator Pitch

Craft your elevator pitch—where you tell someone what you do in less than 30 seconds. Take some time with this, and practice with your family and friends and in front of the mirror. After someone hears your elevator pitch, they should be able to tell others what you do. Make sure you are clear about what you are offering.

Imagine waiting in line with other moms at a sign-up for swim lessons. You start talking with the woman in front of you and the conversation turns to what you do. You are a dog trainer and, without an elevator pitch, you say something like, "Uhmmm, I train dogs, you know sit, stay. I love puppies, they're so cute. It's so much fun to be around them, I just love it." Not much information.

How about, "I have my own dog-training business focused on getting puppies housebroken and getting them to respond to basic commands such as sit, stay, and come. Most new puppy owners struggle with training and my service is here to help them get through the difficult first few months. It's called Lucky Star Training. You can read all about it on my website, luckystartraining.com. May I give you my card?" The response would most likely be, "Wow, I have so many friends who could use you." Or, "I'm getting a puppy next month, can I call you?"

Here's another example. The woman in line asks what you do for work and you say, "I have a business running tag sales in the tri-state area; it's called The Total Tag Sale. Most of my clients are people who are moving, downsizing, or cleaning out estates. Check out my website The-TotalTagSale.com." That actually takes less than 30 seconds, but you are able to impart what you do, who you do it for, and your contact information.

Or, "I have my own cupcake business providing unique cupcakes for all size parties, from children's birthday parties to large charity events. I call my business Crafty Cupcakes and you can see my creations on my Facebook page or on my website, craftycupcakes.com." After this quick introduction to your business, be sure to offer your card. Work to make your elevator pitch casual and conversational. The goal of an elevator pitch is to distill a description of your business venture into one or two simple sentences.

 IN YOUR NOTEBOOK

Draft your elevator pitch. Write and rewrite it until it feels natural and conversational when you practice it with family and friends. And do practice it with family and friends.

Let's take a closer look at the key elements of an elevator pitch. You want your pitch to address:

- The problem (what needs fixing)
- The solution (what you do)
- Who you do it for
- How they can find you

When the mom you talked with in line looks online for The Total Tag Sale or Crafty Cupcakes, she'll find you. This goes back to why it's important to have a descriptive, catchy name that people will remember and why you need a website even if it's just one page with your contact info. So develop your elevator pitch and practice it.

Assignment #2: Ask for Referrals

Don't underestimate the old-fashioned marketing technique of word of mouth. It's extremely powerful. In fact, many moms I've interviewed have done absolutely nothing to market themselves and have an active business just through word-of-mouth referrals. So this week, if you have existing clients, ask your happy customers to refer their friends. You might even offer a discount to current customers if one of their friends becomes a client.

For example, if you are a dog trainer, most clients call you when they have a new puppy and use you for just a few sessions. Your client base is continually turning over, and you have a constant need to get new clients. When you finish training a client's puppy, tell them that if they refer someone who purchases your services, they'll get a gift bag filled with doggie treats, or a free 30-minute refresher session, or some other bonus for referring you to their friends.

If you don't have clients yet, ask your friends and family to refer you. Offer some kind of value or a bonus. Get creative. You could give a Starbucks gift card to the first family member who finds you a client.

 IN YOUR NOTEBOOK

Keep track of orders generated by word-of-mouth referrals. If you offered an incentive, did it make a difference? What worked? What didn't?

Assignment #3: Be a Joiner

By joining groups you'll be expanding the universe of people who could become clients. And it's not just the people in the group; they have friends who could be your clients or customers. Most towns have a variety of groups for everything from dog owners, to mothers of newborns, to runners, to entrepreneurs—you name it, it's out there. Many groups meet on a regular basis. Do a search to find the groups in your area. Look for groups through the Chamber of Commerce, your local library, and the Web. Check out women's associations, school groups, and alumni groups—you get the picture.

Look for a group whose gatherings are attended by members who are your target market. Where you can, join and become an active member. It might be a charity that is run by local moms who could use your service venture or would buy your product. Mom groups are everywhere and a great place to network and share information about your venture. But make sure you are really interested in being a part of the group, and are able and willing to contribute—apart from networking for your business. It's important that you are genuinely interested in what the group is all about.

Join an entrepreneurs' group. Even though members may not be your clients, it's a great way to get support and input. Check out "meetups" around your interests. Meetup.com is an online service that puts like-minded people together. Visit the site and get started. You'll meet others in your field, share ideas, and gain support. Check out meetups of your target audience. If you are really diligent you could probably attend three net-working groups a day—but I'd start off trying a few groups to find which gatherings offer the most value to you.

Be sure that you have your elevator pitch down. Many times, groups specifically set up for networking invite each person to introduce them-selves and tell what they do. Bring plenty of business cards. Other attend-ees are there to meet you and exchange cards. These new contacts should be added to your email list of people to stay in touch with. They may not become clients, but their friends might.

 IN YOUR NOTEBOOK

Keep a list of possible networking groups. If you attend, take notes on which ones work for your venture and which ones don't.

Assignment #4: Spread the Word

Tell everyone you know what you are doing; tell everyone you meet what you are doing. Everyone loves to help a new venture get going, so ask for input and suggestions. Be sure to mention your website address so they can find you.

Public relations (PR) is another area entirely, but you can start small if your budget doesn't allow for hiring someone. This week write your own press release and send it to the local media. You may be able to get the local paper and local circulars to do an article about your new business venture. Call or look online for the correct contact. Look at www.creat-eyourownpressrelease.com to get the format for a simple press release. There is an art to PR and contacts are everything, but generally the local papers and news sites are open to stories about people from town.

The local radio and TV stations may be interested as well. Develop and keep a list of PR contacts and send them updates when you have some interesting news. Start a separate list for PR in your e-letter service. A first press release could feature your introductory and start-up information.

Then you might send another one when you get a big client or help some-one through your venture. Scan the papers to see what they are looking for and develop an angle to your story when writing your press release. For example, a great angle for a nutritional venture might be back to school for the kids and back to fitness for moms. So rather than just talk about your fitness program, you're wrapping it around a seasonal event.

For landscape design, you might write about how to maintain gardens throughout the year, or what to plant in a perennial bed, or what flowers to use for various in-home arrangements. Find a hook to your pitch that connects your product or service to something that will interest readers (or listeners or viewers) rather than simply describing what you're offering. The media are always looking for content—especially local content—and you want to help them see what makes your product or service stand out.

 IN YOUR NOTEBOOK

Keep a list of your PR contacts, organized by media. Update the list peri-odically.

Assignment #5: Find a Fair

Many fairs covering a wide range of interests offer booths for vendors. There is usually a cost to renting a table, so weigh the cost against how many attendees the sponsors expect. And make sure you'll be connecting with your target market. Get feedback from previous vendors to find out about the sponsors and size and type of crowds to expect.

For example, in Stamford, Connecticut, there's an annual fair called the MomEFair. Attendees are local families. Vendors each have a table and the doors are open for a full afternoon with goodie bags and activities for the kids. If your product or service meets the needs of families and moms, this would be a good fit.

You can always attend a fair to gather information and plan to be a vendor the next year if the fit is right. Attending allows you to see what kinds of vendors and attendees the event attracts. Make a note of what the vendors have on their tables and how they present their product or ser-vice. Many have professional signs and tablecloths in their product colors. Some offer samples and candy to get people to stop by their table. And most have a convenient way for attendees to sign up for their newsletter, blog, or Facebook page. If you decide to sign up for a booth or table at one of these venues, make sure you are ready. Many fair sponsors have e-letters so you can get updates on the event.

 IN YOUR NOTEBOOK

Make a list of possible fair venues that would be a good fit for your venture. If you go, take notes on the vendors and attendees, and pay attention to how vendors set up their booths or tables and how they showcase their products or services.

Assignment #6: Donate to a Goodie Bag

It's common at events and meetings for sponsors to give away goodie bags to members and attendees. Find a goodie bag opportunity and create something to donate, whether it's a sample or a postcard with a coupon or bonus. You often don't have to rent a table to donate to the goodie bag. Sometimes you have to pay to be in the goodie bag, but there are plenty of opportunities to donate without having to pay.

Reach out to local charities and groups to find these opportunities. If it's a fit, donate a sample. Make sure your contact info is on the sample. Food and beauty products are ideal for this. If you are offering a service, offer a discount or a free consultation for a first-time client. Be specific about what you are offering. Find out how many items they'll need, when they need them, and where the items need to be delivered.

If you don't have a product sample to offer, you can use one of the business card/logo sites, such as VistaPrint, to create just about anything with your name and logo on it. Everything from pens, to mouse pads, to magnets, to chip clips, to gummy bracelets can be branded. But often you'll need to order large quantities to make it economical. Try an inexpensive donation like a postcard first and measure the payoff before you invest in creating your own goodie bag item.

 IN YOUR NOTEBOOK

Keep a running list of organizations that use goodie bags as part of their promotion efforts. Also keep a list of ways your product or service can be packaged for goodie bags.

Assignment #7: Consider Speaking

It's not for everyone, but offering to give a 15- to 20-minute talk to local groups can help you gain recognition and spread the word about your venture. For example, if you offer a meal service for busy moms, prepare a 20-minute presentation during which you give a demonstration on three easy meals to prep in 30 minutes or less. If you offer a wardrobe consulting business, do a demonstration on putting together some sample outfits. Your talk should be informative, not a sales pitch.

If you decide it's for you, send a note with your availability to the library and local groups who are looking to educate their members. Be sure to practice your speech in front of a group of friends. This is extremely important. Time your talk and get feedback. If this is something you want to do and you feel that your public-speaking skills need improvement, consider joining a Toastmasters group in your area. This organization helps members to improve their speaking skills.

 IN YOUR NOTEBOOK

For every speech or presentation given, analyze your performance. What went well? What could be improved? What kinds of questions did audience members ask?

The bottom line for networking this week is to get out there and spread the word about your venture.

NETWORKING SUCCESS STORIES

Caterina of Cat's Cake Pops did it via mom goups, but that's just one of the avenues to a thriving venture. The following stories show how three other women used networking to build their businesses.

Trade Marks the Spot: Laurie Marshall

When Laurie Marshall started her own business focusing on trademark applications, she couldn't think of a better way to advertise her service than by networking. Her target market is small businesses that are just getting started. She offers a low-priced package to help entrepreneurs with their trademark needs. Speaking and networking at groups for women, start-ups, and small businesses has helped her grow her venture to the point where she's had to hire an assistant.

Sometimes your career can lead you to a venture. That's what happened to Laurie Marshall when she left her corporate job. Laurie had first worked as the in-house trademark counsel for Major League Baseball (MLB). After ten years, she wanted to focus more on her family and left to work part time at a law firm that represents the MLB clubs. A few years later, the law firm had to cut part-timers when the economy slowed down. Laurie was expecting her second child, and this was the perfect time for her to take a break.

However, a couple of weeks later, while she was on the way to the hospital to deliver her baby, Laurie got a call from a team asking, "Can you still handle trademark work for us?" This was her entrée into working for herself. The first MLB club grew to over a dozen clubs, but she still needed to expand her client base to make her business firm viable. With so many people losing their jobs and starting their own businesses, friends, and friends of friends, began to ask Laurie to do trademark work for them. She saw a niche developing around her specialty.

"I wasn't quite sure how to model my business, but I saw a need from start-ups." Laurie cut her prices to appeal to small businesses and her volume grew. "I decided to charge a flat fee for getting a trademark; this includes searching the federal and state trademark database, giving a legal opinion, preparing a trademark application, and handling any nonsubstantive objections with the trademark office." She offered a 30-day turnaround (all for $495). "Some start-ups and small businesses want a ten-day turnaround, and I charge a higher flat fee for this expedited service."

Laurie also saw where larger companies wanted to outsource to save money. "Fifty percent of my business comes from other law firms who know I'm a trademark specialist, and they reach out to me."

How does Laurie get the word out on her niche business? Networking. "I speak everywhere—women's groups, entrepreneurs' groups, schools, panels—anywhere that there is an audience for start-ups and a need for trademark assistance." Laurie developed a 20-minute presentation on trademark law, recommendations, and the application process. She then researched groups that would need her services and contacted them offering a free presentation.

Laurie also began to attend regular meetings of groups that could generate clients. Groups of women entrepreneurs and start-up groups were great sources of new business. She also posts her business on sites that her potential clients frequent, where they are likely to find her. Some of these sites charge a fee for listings, but she generally recoups her investment with just one new client from each source.

Interns are also a big part of helping her grow. "I was able to get interns from the local technical school to help with social media, marketing, and accounting." Additionally, a legal intern from the law school she attended has been invaluable as her business has expanded.

Laurie believes the intern process is great for all concerned—small businesses benefit from what smart, motivated young people bring to their ventures, and interns looking to build their resumés and acquire experience get firsthand professional exposure .

"It's incredibly empowering, never in a million years did I think I'd go out on my own. I could think of every reason not to—yet here I am. That's the irony of the situation."

TAKEAWAY

- Focus on a single area related to your expertise.
- Find a need in the market and fulfill it.
- Set your price at a point that will attract clients.

Nothin' But Granola: Jerri Graham

Sleepless nights led Jerri Graham to create a granola bar using unique combinations of nuts, fruits, and spices. When they quickly sold out at a local coffee shop, she knew she had a viable venture. But getting the word out was key. Jerri donated her product to local charities and joined her local farmers' market to introduce her granola bars to the world.

She is passionate about her granola bars. Finding most granola bars sorely lacking in texture and taste, Jerri Graham set out to create a granola that had texture, crunch, and great flavor. "There was nothing out there that satisfied my personal taste; most granolas were all oats, and there is so much more to offer." When you taste her blueberry, lavender, and cashew bar, you know she's right.

So how did she get into this competitive food product area? When she was in her 20s, Jerri moved from rural Ohio to France, and her world travels began. Working for the Navy as a photographer took her around the globe, and she discovered the many spices and combinations of flavors that Americans sometimes miss. These discoveries stayed with her, and they served her well when her career as a baker began.

Jerry's baking got its start in 2009, when insomnia led her to late-night baking to pass the time. That's when her granola bars were born. Her goal was to create a bar with both flavor and crunch. She came up with four varieties and asked a friend to offer them for sale at her coffee shop. From a basket on the counter, they sold quickly, and customers asked for more.

With that validation, Jerri decided to offer her bars at the weekend farmers' market in her area. She called them *Nothin' But Granola*, a play on the old Saatchi & Saatchi advertising firm motto, "Be nothing but your authentic self." The farmers' market proved to be the best kind of networking. Each week she was not only finding her customers, but also meeting other small vendors who sold their goods at the market. These contacts provided great information on other types of sales venues, information on potential pitfalls to avoid in running a small business, and tips for success. Jerri found that commiserating and sharing information with like-minded vendors was extremely helpful. Joining the Farmer's Market Consortium allows Jerri to meet new customers every Saturday. She also speaks to small groups about how she started her business and showcases her granola at local fairs. Jerri also reaches out to local charities that are looking for items to add to goodie bags for events. She donates minibars, which is a great way to promote her product.

Jerri did all this while she had a job at a magazine. "I had worked for others for many years and didn't like the idea of someone else holding my future in their hands; it was time to do something on my own," she says. Sometimes, one door closes and another opens. When she was laid off from her magazine job, Jerri knew it was time to go to the next level with her granola.

Maybe it was the coconut/chocolate/almond bar, or the ginger/lemon/cashew bar; but whatever the combination, Jerri had a talent for putting the right flavors together and getting the ideal ratio of crunch to chewiness. She found a commercial kitchen and began hiring to ramp up production. Jerri now sells her bars in various locations in Connecticut and

New York and has changed her company's name to Nothin' But Premium Foods, affectionately known as "Nothin' But" by all.

Jerri sees granola as part of an overall plan for healthy eating, often presenting her bars with yogurt and cheeses, which together can make up a satisfying meal. Her creative presentations and passionate delivery when describing her product—"Your tongue is a taste map, and my bars help people travel from the salty edge to the sweet taste and everywhere in be-tween."—have propelled Jerri and her brand toward success.

TAKEAWAY

- Communicate your passion in your description of your product or service.
- Find venues that are appropriate to showcase your product and network there—for example, holiday boutiques, fairs, women's groups, or farmers' markets.
- Donate small samples of your product or your service for goodie bags at charity events.

Mommy Makeup: Debra Rubin-Roberts

When her first baby was a newborn and she was breast-feeding, Debra Rubin-Roberts realized the need to save time when getting herself to-gether. So she created a makeup line specifically for busy moms that can be applied in six minutes. Debra decided networking was key to building her business. She began attending trade shows that focused on beauty and maternity. These trade shows became her go-to marketing plan.

When new mom Debra Rubin-Roberts had to turn down a chance for a dinner out because she couldn't get herself together in time to get back for the next feeding, she had a moment. That was when she realized there was a need for a streamlined makeup process targeted to new moms. She had been a makeup artist for many years and worked in the product develop-ment area with a cosmetics company. "I knew what was involved in creat-ing makeup products, and having a newborn gave me an idea for busy moms."

First she did some hands-on research after that missed night out. "One day when Daisy was napping I worked out a way to do my makeup in less than six minutes, and this became the heart of my new venture." Debra realized that many other busy moms needed a streamlined process for makeup, but still wanted professional results, so she decided to market her application technique and develop the products to go with it as well.

She reached out to her contacts in the business and started to work on developing her line. She called it Mommy Makeup, but anyone who wants to simplify her routine can use the products. "Friends in the business helped me find the right manufacturer." Debra says, "It was important to be made in the United States, and that it be allergy tested, cruelty free, talc free, oil free, fragrance free, and paraben free." It didn't take Debra long to get her requests into the hands of the developers, and while she waited for her product, she worked on packaging and marketing.

Her signature package, called the Pretty-n-Polished Kit, contains six products and a paint by number instruction guide and face chart, all in a smart makeup bag. Users can view a video tutorial online to see how Debra gets herself "pretty n'polished" in just six minutes. Debra says, "The products are makeup-artist quality with quality textures and consistencies, yet are quick and easy to use."

Her next challenge was figuring out how to sell her product. Like so many other women starting their own ventures, she says, "My first sales came from an e-blast I sent to family and friends." Next her husband set up the website, mommymakeup.com. But the real growth came from attending trade shows for beauty and maternity lines. Debra knew that this was the best place to network with the potential buyers for her product. People are more likely to do business with people they have met. As a vendor, Debra set up a table with her products and signage, branded with her venture name and logo. Costs vary for these shows, but in Debra's case they paid off: "At these shows, online retailers loved the line and proposed a deal to offer it on their e-commerce sites." Trunk shows and boutiques where she can network with other vendors and reach her target market are also a big part of her marketing plan.

Now with four employees, Debra works all the time, "But I love that my hours are flexible. Sometimes I work before the kids get up, sometimes after they go to bed, but I can decide what my day looks like." As a sweet homage to her girls and their friends, Debra named the shades in a line of lip gloss after them. What more could any mom ask for? A no-nonsense makeup regimen after her own heart.

TAKEAWAY

- Find trade shows that focus on your product space and decide if it's worthwhile to attend.
- Create effective signage for your table. If your income permits, include branded swag to give away at these events, such as pens, gummy bracelets, and magnets.
- Attend all networking events where your target audience can be found.

———

Now it's time to get your first sale. Week 12 coming up.

twelve

Week 12:
Ka-Ching! Get Your First Sale

When Carolyn Savin started her event design business she didn't have a client, much less a portfolio. She had been making fabulously decorated cookies for years for gatherings of friends and family and was known around town as "the cookie mom." But she realized what she really enjoyed was designing events. Carolyn had been designing her own themed parties for years and people loved them. To get her first clients in this area, and ultimately photos for her online presence, she offered her design service at no charge. She only charged for the materials needed to execute her cool ideas. Providing this free service, she was able to put together her first events for clients and gather photos for her portfolio. From those first clients she got a name for herself as the go-to person for event design and a name and tag line for her new business—Poppyseed Events: "it's the little things . . ."

So, however you can, and even if you do it for free or give away a product or two, your goal this week is to get your first client or sale.

By now, you should be close to getting your first client if you haven't already. You've emailed everyone you know, told everyone you know, set up a website, updated your status on your Facebook fan page, started a Twitter account, created business cards, attended some networking events, and put up flyers.

WEEK 12 ASSIGNMENTS

The focus this week is on getting that all-important first sale.

Assignment #1: Get a Client or Sale

If you don't yet have a client or a potential sale, it's time to find one. Offer your aunt, friend, or neighbor your service at no charge. If you haven't sold one product, donate it to someone who appreciates what you are offering. Donate your item to a charity auction, event, or goodie bag. If you have a baked item, take it to a friend. If you offer an organizational service, clean out your mom's mudroom. If you arrange bookshelves, help your neighbor showcase her travel finds. If you make belt buckles, make one for your sister-in-law. If you offer tag sales, run one for your elderly neighbor.

This is easy, right?

Assignment #2: Get Feedback

Get feedback from your first sale. Take photos, ask for a testimonial, and request that your client or customer refer you. For example, if you are starting a dog-walking business, when your neighbor takes you up on your offer to walk her dog, ask her how the dog liked his exercise. Take photos of the dog and your outings.

If you're starting a wardrobe consulting business, and you help your friend clean out her closet, take photos of outfits you put together for her. Maybe your friend needs a dress for an upcoming wedding or she needs to pack for a cruise. Write about the details of what she needs and ask her to tell you how you helped her. Take notes and get quotes from her.

Assignment #3: Post on Your Website and Social Media Accounts

Everything you do can go on Facebook, on Twitter, and on Pinterest. As you get photos and testimonials, and maybe even press, be sure to put it on your webite as well. If you're offering a family meal service, post photos of finished dishes and make suggestions for healthy snacks.

Followers love the personal side of what you offer. As a wardrobe consultant, the assistance you provide your best friend can provide a multitude of postings. Or you might post outfits you put together for yourself, or outfits you like on celebrities with how to get the same outfit less expensively. The possibilities are endless—for any venture—when you bring your creativity and enthusiasm to the task.

If you offer a food product, post photos of your finished product, your process, your ideas, and your ingredients. Seasonal items and ideas are great to post. It's time to get creative.

 IN YOUR NOTEBOOK

Take notes on your first sale (or sales) and the feedback you gather.

Assignment #4: Put Together a Portfolio

Put all this on your website so that when you want to show someone your work, you can either refer them to the site or take them through it in person or on the phone. You can also put this on an iPad for ease of display. If you plan to email examples, put together photos of your work to send. Create a link to your samples or photos of your service that you can use in your e-letters and in your social media. This may be as simple as linking to your website address where all of your photos are posted.

Before and after photos are great. This is especially true for organizers. Show a messy basement or closet before and then the after shot of the organized space. If you are a dog walker, show a sad dog before and then a happy dog with their doggy friends after. Or if you are starting a child's photography business, show an empty frame and then a frame with a photo of a smiling child. You get the idea. Show how your product or service can help potential clients.

Assignment #5: Celebrate

Has it been 12 weeks already? Time to pop a bottle of bubbly and toast all your hard work. Enjoy the fact that you have created a business venture for yourself to build and enjoy.

FIRST SALE SUCCESS STORIES

You came up with an idea, gave it a name, have begun to tell the world about it—and now it's time to ring the cash register. See how the moms below, like Carolyn Savin of Poppyseed, all used their creativity and imagination to get that first sale.

Younger You e.Oil: Cheryl MacCluskey

When Cheryl MacCluskey finally had her product in hand, she needed to sell it. Creating a natural oil using cold-pressed avocado, she was offering the natural healing benefits of essential oils. But she needed to get her oils in the hands of potential customers. Passing out small samples to friends and family first, Cheryl then hit the spas and left samples of her product. These spas gave e.Oil its first bulk orders.

In her Bikram yoga class, she noticed women putting drops of oil on the edges of their mats and wondered why. Cheryl MacCluskey learned that the women were using essential oils for the calming effects created by their scents. She went on a quest to learn more about the oils and their healing properties.

"I've always been a health nut and practiced yoga every day." Her research confirmed that essential oils and natural skin care products were in keeping with her healthful approach to living; she also learned that there was a long list of chemicals found in the beauty products she was using every day. So she decided to create her own line of skin care products and began with the oils.

Cheryl used cold-pressed avocado oil as her base to create her line. This oil is a natural moisturizer and can be scented with natural fragrances that affect one's emotional and physical well-being. Cheryl's oils, she says, "are organic, paraben-free, and contain no chemicals. They have a renewing effect on your skin and the natural antioxidants in the oils fight against dry, dull, inflamed skin." For a logo, Cheryl chose a dragonfly to symbolize peace, happiness, and new beginnings.

Cheryl began the process of getting her product into potential customers' hands by giving her oils and scrubs to her friends and family so she could get feedback. Cheryl wanted to test her oils and various fragrances to make sure she had a viable product. They loved the product, and not only did this group become loyal buyers but they also shaped future product choices with their input.

Her next step was to reach out to massage therapists, healthcare professionals, and spas. The orders came in. With this positive response, Cheryl now plans to expand her line to include toners, creams, and lotions under the new name "Younger You." She found a friend to help with her website and a college intern to help fulfill orders. Cheryl is busy drumming up orders and has a production company in New Jersey that is ready to deliver the goods.

By putting all these pieces together, Cheryl has put Younger You and e.Oil on the way to becoming a recognized brand in the field of natural beauty products.

TAKEAWAY

- Define your target audience, and then put your product in front of them by delivering free samples.

Olivia & Owen: Christina Lari

Christina Lari couldn't find the high-quality sleepwear she wanted for her young children, so she created her own. Sourcing the perfect cotton, she created her line and ordered samples. Now what? Joining two friends who also had start-up children's lines, the three women ran a pop-up shop in New York City. Pop-up shops take advantage of short-term leases and can be open from two days to three months. This was how Christina got her first sales and created the buzz she needed to jump-start her new venture.

When guests stopped by at bedtime, she wanted her daughter, Olivia, to look nice. But Christina Lari couldn't find the high-quality sleepwear she wanted to dress her two-year-old in—so she created her own. When her mother had brought back beautiful sleepwear from a trip to Europe, Christina noticed the supersoft cotton they were made of. She loved the simple elegance of the pieces and wanted more of them.

But when Christina found nothing similar in the local baby stores, off she went to the fashion district to source the material. "The cotton was the perfect fabric for what I wanted to create but it was difficult to acquire." Finally she found the Pima cotton—from Peru—in Los Angeles and took it, along with her self-created, European-inspired patterns, to a New York City production company.

Christina decided to create a full line of toddler sleepwear imbued with old-world style and charm. She wanted bedtime clothing for her daughter similar to the pieces her mother had brought from Europe, and she figured other mothers would want the same thing. Christina self-funded her first order of samples, not really sure what her next move would be. She was learning the process as she progressed through each step. But she had an advantage. Several of her friends had their own children's wear lines: Kimberly Goodwin with Snapping Turtle Kids and Christin Rueger of Chic Child. These friends offered their insight and assistance.

The three moms decided to run a two-week pop-up shop. For a minimal fee, they rented an empty storefront for two weeks. The women told their network of friends and family and used social media to get the word out. Passersby accounted for a lot of traffic as well. Sharing ideas and stories during their time running the shop gave Christina more ideas for how to grow. A friend of a friend helped her set up a website and get organized for e-commerce. Through word of mouth and good buzz, Christina sold 60 percent of her first run online and was on her way. The venture's name came from her daughter, Olivia, and "Owie" (what Olivia and the other grandkids call Christina's mom). "Owie" turned to Owen, hence the name Olivia & Owen.

With half of her office filled with Olivia & Owen inventory and the other half with real estate files (from her full-time job with her family's real estate development firm), she runs Olivia & Owen in her free time.

"People fell in love with the sleepwear, and I realized I needed help with sales and marketing if I was going to build on my success." So Christina did what many moms do, she went to her network and found a friend with a newborn who had left her full-time job in marketing. Helping Olivia & Owen with sales and marketing turned into a perfect fit for this mom.

Christina has plans to attend the Children's Wear Show, and her goal is to be in stores across the country. She now produces six styles for boys and girls. She says, "I had a vision and made it happen. Sometimes I ask myself, 'What did I do?'"

- Don't be afraid to start a venture in an area where you have no experience. Passion, commitment, and hard work can carry you a long way.
- Pop-up shops are a great way to showcase a product. They can be very inexpensive and sometimes free because landlords want to showcase their available retail space.

Summer Kitchen Bake House: Jennifer McDermott

Using guerrilla marketing techniques (creative and often low-tech ways to get your message to the masses), Jennifer McDermott was able to get her message to the masses. She gave her target market her product—one of her delicious, artfully decorated cookies—and a business card. This started her business.

She was always a baker but not sure how she would create a business venture. Jennifer McDermott loved to create tasty cookies and was a master at decorating them with colorful icing. When you look at her designs you could say she paints with sugar.

She had worked for an art dealer in New York City, but kids and the suburbs gave her a change of direction. Jennifer was looking to use her creativity and wanted to have her own business. When other moms saw the fabulous cookies she created for school snacks and her own children's birthday parties, they wanted her to make her cookies for their parties. A light bulb went off.

She decided to offer her custom cookie baking service to other nursery school moms. And to market her new business venture, Jennifer enclosed a cookie and a business card in a cellophane bag and dropped them off in the mailboxes of the moms from her son's nursery school. Her son even assisted in cookie deliveries while still in his car seat. This guerrilla tactic garnered clients right away

Jennifer then found a local charity and offered to donate an elegant, appropriately themed cookie to each attendee. Everyone got not only one of her beautiful cookie creations, but also a flyer with her information. This technique literally started her business. Now her small cookie venture is a full-fledged bakery: Summer Kitchen Bake House.

TAKEAWAY

- Be creative in finding ways to get your product and information into the hands of your target customers.
- Donate your item to a local charity to gain exposure.

———

Congratulations on your first sale!

The next chapter is all about making time for your venture so you can reap the rewards that it generates. You know how your venture makes you feel; now you'll see what other venture moms are saying.

IV

VENTURE PATHS
TO SUCCESS

thirteen

Make the Time and Reap the Rewards

Congratulations! You've completed the 12-week journey, and now you're running your own venture. It's time to make a plan to continue to market and promote your venture. If you're like most women who run their own businesses, you love what you're doing and wake up each day wanting to work toward more success.

As busy women raising children, often we find it difficult to make time for the things that give us our fulfillment and happiness (your venture). Having a business venture has so many rewards that making time for that venture should be at the top of your list of things to do. Here are some suggestions and, yes, a few more assignments to keep you on task so you can experience all the benefits of having your own business.

MAKING THE TIME

Finding time for your venture has probably proven to be a challenge. So how can you carve out time for your projects?

First, go back through the marketing topics in Week 8 through Week 12. Pull out what has been working and make a list of what you need to continue to do to garner sales. Prioritize. Figure out what to make a priority and then allocate time for it. Since you've been in the program you have found time, but setting aside an hour a day to work on marketing and promotion will move you further along your path.

Eliminate Distraction

The home office can be a trap. Most women like you will walk toward your desk and see a pillow out of place on the couch. While arranging the pillows, you see dust under the rug and get the mini-vac to pick it up. When you put the mini-vac away, you see a load of laundry to put in and the phone rings. After a 10-minute conversation with your friend you remember to call for a doctor's appointment, and then the dog needs to be let in and needs water. As you approach your computer, the doorbell rings and it's the guy who's there to clean the furnace. When you show him the basement you see several bags that need to go to Goodwill, so you carry those upstairs and decide to gather a few more items so you can have everything to take with you when you drive to the Goodwill drop-off location. You walk by your kids' rooms and see the beds need making. It goes on and on, and before long your day is over and you've done nothing to move your venture along.

You must drop everything else and focus on your venture. Leave the laundry in the basket, the clothes on the floor, the phone unanswered, the dishes in the sink. Focus on your venture.

Adopt the 1–5–10 Plan

Here's the plan. To complete the 12-week program, you've been successful at carving out the time you needed to complete your assignments. Now you need to keep that momentum going. Maybe you already have an hour or more set aside for your venture. But if not, start Week 13, the first week with your venture in play, by spending an hour on your new venture. To make this time, maybe you get up an hour earlier. Maybe you cut out a TV show. Maybe you exercise an hour less or skip a lunch with friends. If you have a full-time job, maybe you work on your venture during a lunch break or on the weekend.

As you gain steam, you'll want more time. Practice will make it happen. Make an appointment with yourself in your scheduler and stick with it. Once that hour has become part of your routine, work up to five hours a week. You will be doing something you love and are passionate about so it won't seem like a sacrifice.

Then move to 10 hours. Women are amazing at getting more done when they have less time. If you spend 10 hours a week on one thing, you will get somewhere. Here are some other tips:

- Set a schedule and stick with it.
- Only work on your venture—no phone calls, emails, laundry, dishes.
- Turn the TV off, or record your favorite shows to watch later.
- Get a babysitter if you have to, and lock yourself in your office.

If you left your house for work, all of those household tasks would be there when you return. Approach your home office hours the same way. Walk to your desk, into your office, or to your phone as if you are walking into an office away from home.

Compartmentalize

When you work, only work. When you're with your kids, focus on them only. When you're with your friends or husband, don't allow your mind to wander to all the things you want to do with your venture. These people know when you are distracted.

If you run your own businesses, you know you can get phone calls and emails at any time of day or night and there is no such thing as a vacation. Try turning off your phone. If you can work toward separating your family life from your work life, you, your family—*and* your clients—will be much happier.

REAPING THE REWARDS

You've created a venture and carved out the time from your overbooked schedule with your family—now it's time to reap the rewards. Having a venture is incredibly inspiring to the women who've done it. Emotionally, there is a high from creating something out of thin air with your own persistence and hard work.

Many women start their ventures because they are looking for fulfillment outside of motherhood. Or they left high-powered jobs to stay home and raise their children. Or they have a job that doesn't provide the happiness they desire from their work. But whatever the reason, the moms who start ventures feel really great about themselves. These before and after comments from venture moms should inspire you to make the time you need—so you can reap the rewards.

BEFORE

- I want to start something for me.
- I don't like my job anymore.
- I can't spend all of my days working out, playing tennis, and having lunch.
- I don't want to volunteer; I want to make money.
- I want to volunteer and help other people.
- I want to take my husband to an event that's about me rather than just going to all his work events.
- It's my last chance to do something big. I'm going to be 70 years old soon.
- I'm free from 8:00 A.M. until 4:00 P.M. every day. What can I do for my fulfillment?
- I want a career but I want to be free after 3:00 to be with my kids.
- I want something I can involve my kids in.
- I want to start a venture my son can help me with.
- I used to have a career to talk about. I'm tired of talking about what I made for dinner last night.
- It's not about the money; I want to feel that I created something.
- It's about the money.
- I want a creative challenge.
- I want an identity outside of being a mom.

AFTER

- I'm doing something I love to do.
- I don't make a lot of money, but the happiness I get from it is priceless.
- The new people I've met through my venture are so interesting.
- I have something really cool to talk about with my husband and friends.
- My kids help me run my business.
- I'm free for my children after 3:00 every day.
- I have a huge opportunity to choose what I want to do.
- I can ask my husband to attend an event related to my venture rather than just attending his events.
- I started by spending just two hours a week and now I'm making enough money that I can stop working for someone else.
- My kids are so proud of me; I'm so proud of me.
- I can't wait to get up in the morning and have time to do this thing I love.
- I'm having so much fun.

It's amazing how starting a business can transform a life. Find your passion and pursue it. If you have a passion, you are alive. Psychologists encourage parents to foster their children's passions. It promotes self-esteem. The same holds true for moms.

Imagine how you'd feel if in addition to being a great mom, your friend could introduce you saying, "Meet my neighbor. She _____." What do you want to fill in the blank with? She designs jewelry. She has her own landscaping business. She's a caterer. She's an amazing event planner. She runs the local shelter. She works with an architect. She's a photographer.

I believe that women need to fill in the blanks for themselves. The one thing I've heard from all of the moms I've interviewed is that the pursuit of their passion provides fulfillment.

The following chapters in Part IV share stories of ventures in specific areas. Read them all to garner nuggets of information to use in your venture.

fourteen

Serving Up Food and Drink

Food ventures can be big winners for moms who have an item they want to market. If you bake an item that your friends and family love, you can turn it into a business venture. There is a fairly clear path for a fledgling food business. Most food ventures start out in the home kitchen, where you'll need a permit to make and sell items. Cooking in your own kitchen allows you to start with as little overhead as possible and test the market. Come up with a cute name and packaging and then sell to your circle of friends and family. Patty Reis, founder of Pattycakes, did just that. She is now the one baker in her hometown to call when the occasion calls for a special cake.

To get started, check with your state to see what regulations govern the sale of food made in a residential kitchen. These state laws will guide you in terms of what you can sell, how much you can sell, and to whom you can sell. Many states require a label with the ingredients listed on the package and a statement that the food was made in a home kitchen. Most states will have the guidelines listed on the Web. Starting a food business from a home kitchen is the best way to test the market before gearing up and investing in renting a commercial kitchen, if that is the path you choose; selling from home may be enough, which is a decision you can make as you go.

Online sales are governed by state laws as well. But setting up a website and a shopping cart is a great way to grow your food business. And, of course, farmers' markets feature multiple food items. The cost of setting up a table will vary, but it's a great way to test the public's interest in your product before you invest more in your venture. So many mom-owned ventures got started at farmers' markets and went on to Whole Foods and beyond.

FOOD VENTURE PATH

Food and drink ventures are a big part of small ventures that moms start. If you have a food or drink item to share with the world, your journey might go something like this:

- Develop a food product that gets consistently positive feedback from family and friends.
- Come up with a name, packaging, and pricing.
- Check your state's regulations governing sale of food made in a residential kitchen and license your home kitchen.
- Sell to your circle of acquaintances.
- Get placement at small local stores.
- Sell at your local farmers' market.
- Rent commercial kitchen space, if necessary.
- Expand your store placement.
- Go for placement at national brand stores (Whole Foods and other retailers have links on their sites with information about product submission).

FOOD VENTURE SUCCESS STORIES

You can start a food venture by following the 12-week program outlined in this book. If you are an accomplished cook or baker, start by asking others what you make that they love. Then, go through each week of the program, and by the end of Week 12 you should find yourself with a business. See how these moms got their start—you could be next.

Pattycakes: Patty Reis

With her grandmother as her biggest influence, Patty Reis loved to bake cakes from the time she was in grade school. Baking cupcakes for her own grade-schooler's bake sale led to a new venture. The cupcakes were so well received that friends started to ask her to bake for their kids' birthdays. A treasure chest cake she made for her son became a favorite. Three years ago she got a call from someone who wanted to order a cake. "But I don't have a business," Patty responded. "You make cakes, right, and I'll pay you," said the caller, and Patty was in business.

Patty's donations to local charities, including the Darien Nature Center, where she created a mommy hedgehog cake and baby hedgehog cupcakes, led to rave reviews. And not only were her cakes a wonder to look at, they were delicious. One woman who enjoyed Patty's devil's food cake with dark chocolate ganache filling came up to her and said, "I don't eat cake and I licked the plate. It was that good!"

Baking at night, with cakes sometimes coming out of the oven at midnight and icing going on at 2:00 A.M., Patty doesn't mind cheating sleep to deliver a cake that was baked just a few hours earlier. Her grandmother's influence keeps Patty's style rooted in the 1950s, with simple batter recipes and buttercream frostings. Patty is a stickler for freshness, and she is true to what she knows and loves. Her passion is to be in the kitchen covered in confectioners' sugar and she loves visiting bakeries wherever she goes to get ideas and inspiration. "It makes me so happy and baking is something I really enjoy."

If she were to picture herself six or seven years into the future, when her 16-year-old daughter and 14-year-old son are in college, she would be wearing an apron and standing in the storefront of her own cake business. Patty's been asked to supply local cafés with her baked goods but she knows she needs to co-op a commercial kitchen to move to that level. She is exploring the idea, but for now she stays quite busy baking for birthdays, anniversaries—even a wedding she tried to turn down. The bride insisted: "Your cake is so delicious, it's all I want." She baked that cake and even got a thank-you call from the bride on her honeymoon. Patty's kids love to help ice cupcakes and assemble orders, making Pattycakes a true family venture.

Jen Maher Food: Jen Maher

What started as helping a friend with a venture turned into her own venture. Jen Maher had worked in finance, but she left that field when she had children. Always into cooking and food, Jen went back to school to study nutrition. "My mother was not into cooking, and I was determined to make great healthy meals for my family." Her education in nutrition really made her think about what she and her family were eating.

Jen developed a reputation among her friends for feeding her kids delicious, nutritious meals. When her friend Mollie Boyle asked her to help her with her nutritional counseling business, Jen decided to give it a try. Mollie runs four nutritional cleanses a year with the goal of ridding her clients' diets of gluten, sugar, and dairy. Mollie realized her clients wanted to continue their new food lifestyle after the cleanses and needed access to prepared foods. She felt Jen was the perfect person to recommend.

Jen said she would try the idea and, after checking her state's regulations and ensuring she was in compliance, began to create and offer some enticing dishes from her home kitchen. Mollie's clients then became Jen's clients. With each cleanse that Mollie did, Jen's customer base grew. "I set up a website and added kids' meals too, finding a big demand for gluten-free meals for kids." Without planning to start a venture, Jen was in business.

Jen's menus have a balance of antioxidants, macronutrients, and micronutrients, and in the kids' items she incorporates hidden vegetables at every opportunity. She also came up with a signature dish with inventive packaging: a salad in a mason jar. Clients love the wide range of menu choices she offers for healthy eating. Jen's business has grown to the point where she's had to hire a prep cook and a driver to deliver meals. Her creations arrive in a cooler bag on clients' front stoops. Customers must order in advance and can buy lunches or dinners for one or many, for one day or several, or for the week.

What's her edge? Jen says, "Not only are my meals custom-made, but they are really delicious and healthy at the same time." Jen believes that once someone decides to change their lifestyle, eating this way is easy. "And I'm here to make it easier by providing meals to go."

"I always wanted my own business but would never have just created this if it hadn't fallen into my lap." Jen's business has grown so much she is looking into securing a commercial kitchen. How does she feel about her new venture? "When someone emails me to say that the goat cheese wrap, or whatever Jen Maher creation they've just had, was so delicious, it feels so gratifying. I love to make people happy with food."

Sister Sweets: Kinsey, Kate, Charlotte, and Elizabeth Ferguson

What do three sisters do with another snow day and no school? The oldest sister Kate says, "Let's make cupcakes." The middle sister Charlotte agrees but realizes they don't have boxed cake mix. "Let's make them from scratch," they decide. So the girls head to the Internet to get recipes. Their mom Kinsey is thrilled that the girls have found something to do on their day off other than watch TV.

After trial and error, the girls had three yummy flavors of cupcakes. Now, who to share them with? They trekked through the snow to their neighbor's house to share their sweets and were thrilled to hear the response, "These are so good you should sell them." Tromping back home through the snow, the girls roped their younger sister, Elizabeth, and mom into the act, and spent the day naming their venture Sister Sweets and making business cards. Over the next week they knocked on more doors and went to other neighbors' houses dropping off cards with samples of their new creations. They were in business.

After a couple of orders came in, Kinsey got the girls organized. Buying supplies in bulk and gathering the right tools for baking were the next steps. When the hand mixer broke, the girls netted a new KitchenAid mixer as a gift from their Aunt Wendy. Kinsey helped the girls determine what to charge and made a schedule. Working around school and the activities of a 12-, 15-, and 17-year-old was a feat.

The girls did more research and added new flavors—espresso with chocolate icing, apple cinnamon with apple cream cheese frosting, and coconut with key lime frosting. They took their cards to school and teachers became a big source for orders. They added mini cupcakes to their menu and got orders for events as varied as ladies' luncheons, kids' birthday parties, athletic team banquets, and bridal showers.

Over the summer, through a neighbor's referral, a local sweet shop hired the girls to do the cupcakes every weekend for store parties. "This is so great," Kate says, "I always wanted my own business and never thought it would be cupcakes. But it's something feasible and we've made it profitable."

How did Kinsey feel? Seeing her girls learn to be entrepreneurs was wonderful, but seeing the girls bond and work as a team was the real gift. Kinsey says, "The business gives the girls a sense of accomplishment. I'm there to help with the logistics, packaging, and financing, but the girls make and ice all the cupcakes." Hosting a sampling party for friends in town brought in more orders and helped to broaden the selection of cake flavors and icings.

"It's a cohesive effort and the girls make their own spending money, which is great given the economy." Kinsey says, "I love seeing the girls learn to balance homework and other priorities. This is teaching them a valuable lesson that they can carry with them." The girls used their profits to pay mom back for the baking tools she bought, and they were in the black and looking forward to filling lots of orders—for holidays, special events, whatever opportunities come their way. Sister Sweets' orders came from word of mouth. The girls have gotten older, and, with two of them off to college, their baking venture has faded—but the lessons they learned from it will be with them forever. Future venture moms, without a doubt!

What's your food item? Do you have a secret family recipe? Is there something you make that others rave about? It's time to craft a venture around your cooking talent. Follow the path these women have taken and get started.

In the next chapter, you'll read about how easy it can be to start a successful service venture.

fifteen

Service Ventures

Whether it's setting up websites, creating photo books for special occasions, or teaching an exercise class, there's practically no limit to the talents or skills that can be developed into a service business venture. Think about what women do in your community—everything from dog walking, to running tag sales, to setting up websites. Moms plan parties, organize basements, give computer help, create outfits, design rooms, assist with personal finances, plant gardens, and countless other things. Any of these activities can be developed into a profitable and fulfilling service ventures.

Many service ventures start with a mom doing something exceptionally well for herself. Then her friends ask her to do the same for them. Word spreads and before long she's asked by others to help them out too. This is the time to consider forming your own venture—turning the thing you love to do into something someone will pay you to do.

Service ventures can be some of the easiest ventures to start. Often a service business can be kicked off with one mass email to your friends and family. And these ventures typically have the lowest start-up costs. All of the marketing can be set up on the Web for a very small outlay of cash.

SERVICE VENTURE PATH

Do you have a skill or talent that others would pay for? Do you see a need in your community for a particular service? Have you come up with a unique service idea that will help improve people's lives? If so, your path to a service business venture may look like this:

- If you have a unique skill or talent that others would pay you to provide for them, consider turning it into a venture.
- Brand your venture: Come up with a name, tag line, logo, colors, and a price for what you want to offer.
- Set up a contact point, whether by phone, email, or website—or all three.
- Tell everyone you know what you are offering by email, social media, and word of mouth.

Many service ventures can be scaled over time or right away. Scaling a service venture can be more complicated than scaling a product venture, but the rewards can be commensurate with the investment of time and money. To scale a service venture you may have to consider hiring people to do what you do or franchise your idea.

SERVICE VENTURE SUCCESS STORIES

Skills, talents, and a good idea allowed each of the moms below to build their service businesses, two on a small local scale and one with a broader reach and larger investment. You can too.

The RZ Connection, Moving Specialist: Randi Hutton

Moving from one house to another is one of the top ten most stressful things in life, so wouldn't it be great to have help with the whole process? Randi Hutton had the same thought, and she created a venture around it. Formerly in charge of acquiring screenplays and films for a large company, Randi had left to work for herself. Turning to real estate so she could have flexibility, Randi says the downturn in the market in 2008 led her to expand her services. "I didn't want all my efforts in one area. I saw how stressful it was for people to move and I wanted to help with that transition."

To garner new business, Randi has reached out to and developed relationships with local real estate firms. She provides a 20-minute presentation on her services to the brokers so they know what she can do for their clients. This is her biggest source of new customers and her prime area for networking.

Randi's first step with a client is to hold a meeting to establish a timeline for the move. "My clients heave a huge sigh of relief after this meeting. They realize they have a plan and know the timing for each step." Randi knows that the long list of details to figure out in every move—from how many boxes will be needed, to who is packing, to what needs to be sold, stored, or given away—is a source of stress for anyone planning a move. Randi's goal with each client is to manage that long list of details, make sure everything gets done, and to alleviate some of the stress. "I always recommend purging unneeded items. When a client can get rid of things they don't need in the new house, it takes a huge weight off their shoulders. Not only do they gain physical space but also mental and emotional space."

"I had one client who wanted to leave her old house, go on vacation, and come back to her new house with everything unpacked and ready to go." Randi oversaw the entire process, from finding the right mover, to meeting the mover and managing the packing up, to meeting the mover in the new house and supervising the unpacking and the placement of furniture.

Randi has an organized approach. "I create a drawing of each room with the client, determining where all the furniture would go. I help with the kitchen too, getting guidance from the client. Most people know how they want things to be placed in their kitchen depending on their own needs. Convenience is key." She also likes to suggest that clients organize things in the old house by where they will go in the new house. "And I can work within any budget. Sometimes just a timeline meeting is all a client will need; others want me to do everything while they are away." She says the timeline is essential in giving a client peace of mind and a path.

Randi's family is on board with her venture. Her husband designed the website and even her 20-year-old son is part of the business. The "R" in The RZ Connection comes from Randi and the "Z" is from her son's name, Zachary. "He likes to be involved and jumps in to help when I need him."

Organizing and planning a move gives Randi a great sense of satisfaction. "It's very rewarding to see a house become a home to my clients."

The Local Vault: Betsy, Pat, Julie, and Joannie

This venture was born out of necessity. When Julie couldn't sell various pieces of unwanted furniture and accessories her frustration prompted her to bring it up when she ran into her friend Betsy at the grocery store. The two women batted around some thoughts and figured that, "Surely we can come up with a way to sell this furniture." The two decided they would meet with two other friends who could help them flesh out their idea for Julie and maybe others too.

When Betsy Perry, Patricia Espinosa, Julie Rubich, and Joannie Buhrendorf all got together, they looked at the One Kings Lane business model and thought they could combine a tag sale with a consignment shop, but do it all online. They realized they would need some serious technology to make it happen. A referral led them to a local development team that could create what they envisioned.

Because there were four partners, they formed an LLC. The women met with the developers to build a site that would offer furniture, lamps, and accessories on consignment, exclusively online. Their edge: they would have specific vignettes made up of the items each client wanted to sell and then break them out individually with descriptions and prices. Like a consignment shop, the women would take 40 percent and give the seller 60 percent. It would be a sophisticated way to repurpose things. "People are looking for older, high-quality pieces and want to rein in consumption by reusing things rather than buying new."

They thought how easy it would be to have the items stay at the client's home and simply take photos of the pieces each client wanted to sell. Joannie had high-end photography equipment and the women invested in lighting so the photos on their website would be high quality. Now what to call their new venture?

Julie thought of the word "vault" because it reminded her of the old Loehmann's days when the best designer clothes were in the back of the store in a room called The Vault. Patricia says, "That's where all the good stuff was. We added the word 'local' since we would be offering local finds."

With a name, photography equipment, and a website, the women set out to find clients with upscale furniture and other housewares to sell. "We found clients easily though word of mouth. We like to have at least ten things that we can use to create a vignette. Each client has a storefront of sorts on the site." The Local Vault offers flash sales to let shoppers know the items have a set time to be on the site. Once the time limit is up, the items won't be available. If things don't sell, the client keeps them. If they sell, pickup is arranged.

It's a family affair, Betsy says, "Our IT guy is 12 years old and jumping on the trampoline right now." Joannie's daughter helped them set up on Facebook and they got over 100 Likes almost immediately. The women added other social media and provide a weekly newsletter showcasing current sales.

Each woman has her own strengths and talents to bring to the venture. They say, "It was scary to launch. We were insecure about putting ourselves out there, but we felt that we'd all jump in together. That made it easier." The Local Vault has caught the eye of a local venture funding group—who knows, the "local" may be expanding to other locales.

JoyRide: Amy Hochhauser, Debbie Katz, and Rhodie Lorenze

Lamenting the lack of a boutique cycling studio in their area led three women to a big venture. Amy Hochhauser, a self-described "recovering" attorney, had moved to Westport, Connecticut, when her second son was three. While having lunch one day with her friend Debbie Katz, she said, "I wish we had a great spinning studio here. Someone should open a boutique spinning place in town . . . We should open a spinning place in town!"

These women knew from their circle of friends that there were many other women like themselves who didn't want to join a full-service gym just for a cycling class. And they felt that a studio that focused on cycling would be able to hire the best instructors and offer a higher quality of classes.

Both women had turned to spinning to relieve stress and maintain fitness physically and mentally and loved it. Debbie had been in advertising but wanted a career that was more in line with her current lifestyle.

Not one to sit still when she has an idea, Amy started to ruminate on how this might happen. Late one night, when she couldn't sleep for thinking about it, she began to Google everything she could on spinning classes. "I found a guy in Boston who consults with people who want to start spinning studios. This was the perfect person to talk with." They reached out to him right away and starting thinking of a name for their future studio. She and Debbie wanted it to be a happy and welcoming place for clients. So by combining a feeling of joy (and Amy's grandmother's name) with an action—ride—they landed on JoyRide.

Amy and Debbie's venture was still in its infancy and they weren't sure if they could pull it off, but the two moms kept moving forward. They felt the name had real value and since Amy was a lawyer, she filed for a trademark and formed an LLC. "We then hired the consultant to help us with the basics, which included space requirements, a budget, and management details." Amy and Debbie found this extremely helpful but they realized they were thinking of something larger. "The consultant was great. We took the structure he gave us and expanded on it."

They continued their research and planning. Since this was not an inexpensive venture, they knew they needed capital. They drafted a short business plan and met with everyone they knew. "Borrowing was not an option, so we had to find investors. Lots of people said we couldn't do it, but we had the commitments we needed for our first studio in one week."

The investors turned out to be local people who believed in what they were building. They found them through word of mouth. Amy and Debbie told everyone they knew what they needed. They got contacts and recommendations from their friends and from friends of friends. They also reached out to known business people who were interested in fostering local businesses.

About this time, the consultant called to say that a spinning instructor from Westport, Connecticut, had called him about opening a studio. "He thought it would be a good fit for us. An instructor was the missing piece. Debbie and I worked out, but we weren't instructors." When Amy heard it was Rhodie Lorenze, one of the most successful spinning instructors in the area, she knew it was meant to be.

They met for coffee, shared their ideas, and this is when they knew it was going to happen. The three women became partners with all of the legal documents required, including exit strategies. "You don't want to have this big a venture and not know what would happen if things change for one of the partners."

Eight months after the idea, JoyRide offered its first spinning class. "We were surprised and pleased by the support from friends who came—it was awesome." The women relied on social media to get the word out. Spinners followed their instructors, which brought in clients. The lease they were able to secure gave them more room than they needed, so they have an extra room for other classes. "The spinning instructors also teach Pilates, JoySculpt, and JoyCircuit. Never did I think I'd be running an exercise studio but once I get my mind set on an idea, I won't stop. I knew if we didn't do it, someone else would and the timing was perfect," says Amy. All of the names are unique to them and trademarked—JoyRide, JoySculpt, and JoyCircuit. They have set the business up for expansion by branding everything they offer.

JoyRide just opened its second studio in Darien, Connecticut. Amy says, "I think we've been successful because JoyRide focuses on the mind–body connection, encouraging riders to stay positive and tap into their mental strength." Rhodie's clients thrive on her playlist. She says, "I love to offer a challenging ride and engage with my riders." The best part for the three women: "We love the community among us as owners and formed with our instructors and our clients. This is our extended family."

Service ventures can be large or small, but whatever their size, they present great opportunities for sharing your skills and growing a business. So take advantage of your talents and make them work for you and others.

———

Moms are major problem solvers and creating products to use in raising their children is a big venture area. In the next chapter you'll read about several moms who've created a product for children and built a business with it.

sixteen

The Mother of All Ventures: Children's Products

Mothers are creators and problem solvers. And over the course of their children's lives, when they're faced with the never-ending list of things they need to make life easier, more fun, and more organized, they often come up with unique solutions.

Their creative solutions can lead enterprising moms to create business ventures they never dreamed possible. Whether it's a snap-on bib that can be changed easily or a phone clip for a stroller, when a mom finds that she needs something that is not currently on the market or she creates a better version of something that is, she may have a business venture.

CHILDREN'S PRODUCT VENTURE PATH

If you create something that solves a problem for your family, and others say they love it and want one too, consider making it into a venture.

Children's product developers—mom or otherwise—often travel the path below:

- Research the viability of your product (see Chapter 3).
- Test your product in a focus group.
- Brand your product: develop a name, tag line, logo, colors, and pricing.

- Create a website to showcase your product.
- Use social media to spread the word.
- Research and find out how to create more product on a larger scale so you'll have a plan if sales take off.
- Take your product to market through trunk shows, farmers' markets, pop-up shops, small local shops, and then possibly large chain stores.

If you are developing a children's product, you should probably do what Carla Palmer did (you'll meet her below): take it to a focus group—a great way to test the waters before you spend a lot of money on something that may have issues you are not aware of. Here's how you can set up a focus group with little outlay.

Ask all of your friends in your target group to try your product and give you feedback. In Carla's case, her playgroup became her focus group. If your friends are not your target market, find a group who is by finding one person who meets the criteria through a friend's referral. Then ask that person to ask *her* friends to try your product. Generally you'd offer your product at no charge; most people will give you feedback on a free item. Have a gathering at your home or a coffee shop or another appropriate place—your public library may have meeting rooms that you can reserve for free or for a minimal fee—if you want to watch the group trying your product and witness their reactions in person. You can also mail or deliver your product and ask for verbal or email feedback.

CHILDREN'S PRODUCT SUCCESS STORIES

Great examples of this path are found in stories you've read in previous chapters including the Texthook (Chapter 2), Mommy Makeup (Chapter 11), Tuckadream Pillows (Chapter 4), and many others. Read how three more moms came up with an idea to solve a problem and then created a venture around it.

Snapping Turtle Kids: Kimberly Goodwin

If you've ever tried to change a baby girl's diaper while she's wearing a wet bathing suit, you know it's not easy. That's what Kimberly Goodwin was doing when she realized there was a need for bathing suits with snaps.

These would allow moms to easily change a girl's diaper without taking off the whole wet bathing suit. Kim had no formal fashion background; she had worked in marketing and creative services for *Lucky* magazine. However, while there she had constant contact with fashion people in production and manufacturing.

After a three-month maternity leave, Kim was lucky enough to go back part time, three days a week. So on the other two days, she started researching the manufacturing of bathing suits for babies. "When I told my sister, who was a fashion design major in college, what I wanted to do, she said I was crazy. But once I got started, I knew I couldn't turn back."

While developing her product was done over a period of months, Kim pushed ahead with other aspects of her venture during that time so she was ready to launch when she had her product. This included naming her company, crafting a logo, and building a website.

"I thought about how shoppers would find me with a Google search and I figured moms would remember the snapping part and find me with my name, so I came up with Snapping Turtle Kids."

Kim sourced five fabrics and designed two bathing suit styles for girls in sizes 3 months up to 3T (toddler). Now she had a decision to make. Wanting to focus all her time on her new Snapping Turtle Kids swimsuits, she left the magazine job and worked freelance, but her heart was now in her new venture. Kim searched out and found a U.S. production company that offered the kind of quality she required. "Production cost is a bit more, but when retailers hear that they are made in the United States, they understand. It makes a difference and consumers care that my line is made here."

Self-funding her venture, she was able to order 50–100 pieces of each design in all eight sizes. Now what? "I decided to go big and get a booth at the big children's wear show." It was a three-day commitment so her mom came in to help with her child. "My friends said I'd be lucky to get a couple of business cards at the show . . . I sold out of almost all of my swimsuits and got orders from six retailers in upscale markets."

Kim immediately launched her website with e-commerce. Buyers could now find suits, hats, and coverups online. Social media took her to the next level. Reaching out to mommy bloggers, she was covered nationally and successfully handled the PR and marketing herself. Her basement and an extra bedroom in her apartment became her stockroom and office, and her sales grew rapidly.

With this growth, establishing an office outside of her home became more practical. Now she needed some help. Kim found two interns from FIT, the fashion school in New York City. One intern was majoring in the business side of fashion and one was majoring in children's wear—both a perfect fit. "They help out three days a week, which has been a lifesaver, but the majority of the time, it's all me."

For a personal touch, Kim puts a handwritten note in each order. "Some customers are shocked but I want them to know how much I appreciate their order, especially since I'm a new company." This attention to detail has helped her grow from 5 to 25 stores in six months, and she often asks herself, "What did I get myself into?"

"I have great flexibility, but I'm always working even if it's thinking about ways to grow my company." With requests to expand her line up to size 6 and into boy's suits, she is on her way.

Cheekie Charlie: Carla Palmer

When Carla Palmer's baby was teething, bibs were a necessity but she couldn't find something that was stylish and functional at the same time. "I told my husband I can do this better and we started brainstorming. I wanted to create something unique."

Carla had been in brand design before leaving her career to be a stay-at-home mom. When she thought of the idea to create a bib set that would go with white "onesies," Carla envisioned a set of three bibs in different fabrics that could be snapped on as necessary without having to change the whole outfit. One day at a fabric store, Carla picked up a business card for a seamstress.

"Turns out she was a sweet grandma and I took my seven-month-old daughter, Charlie, with me when I first met her. We got together at a Starbucks so I could show her what I wanted her to sew for me." The grandma was a patternmaker and she set out to create a prototype for Carla. "But she wasn't the person who could produce the numbers I needed." Carla searched for a manufacturer who could and ended up finding a company in Minneapolis.

"When I was looking for the right people, a friend who had started a baby product company became my mentor of sorts. She offered great tips, business suggestions, and needed resources." It's always friends and family who can make it all happen and come together. Carla sent her prototype to the company in Minneapolis and several iterations went back and forth before the sample was as she envisioned it. There was only a minimal charge to get the samples made, which Carla funded herself.

Carla then hosted some focus groups with moms to get input and see what would resonate with her target market. Her focus group members consisted of the moms in her playgroup and friends of friends, so there was no outlay of cash for getting her the feedback she needed. "This was so helpful to see the product on actual babies and in use." One mom told her, "As soon as I strapped my four-month-old into his car seat the other day, he spit up. No problem! I just unsnapped the snap-on bib and gave him a new one."

She chose three different patterned bibs for her first set and now she was ready to place an order with the manufacturer. "It was scary to order in bulk. I was never in marketing." And now she needed a name. With a British husband who had always used the word "cheeky" and even called their daughter cheeky Charlie, Carla thought Cheekie Charlie was the perfect name for her new venture.

Carla decided to start selling online and through trunk shows. Her husband helped create her website and a shopping cart; now she was in business. To get started, she organized a launch party where she invited every mom she knew. The overwhelming response and number of sales solidified her idea. "That was great validation. I learn something new about marketing every day. And by reaching out to mommy bloggers and newspapers, I even got press coverage."

Then Carla had another discovery. Carla began personalizing T-shirts for her daughter Charlie and when other moms liked them so much, she decided to expand her brand. "I love that I have my own business and I can't wait to tell Charlie, when's she old enough, how I did it all with her as my inspiration."

The Enchanted Bookery: Susannah Altman

The only gifts her new son received that he didn't rapidly outgrow were books. When Susannah Altman left the field of clinical psychology to raise a family, she never thought a baby gift would lead her to a business venture. "Coming from a family of avid readers, books became the gift of choice for my friends' new babies. I created a book basket for a shower and the moms there raved about it and asked me to make these gifts for them to give. This is when I realized I had the seed of a new business."

So Susannah set out to get organized. She started with a name and a logo. "I wanted the name to tell what I did and give a feeling of whimsy, so I came up with The Enchanted Bookery." Next she began to set up accounts with the publishers of her favorite children's books. To do this she contacted the publishers and applied for a wholesale account so she could order in bulk and get the books at a discount.

Then she needed to do some marketing and started building a mailing list that included her friends and family. This was in 1996, before the Internet was so widespread, so Susannah sent out mailers about her new business to potential clients. Orders started to come in from this process, from word of mouth, and from gift recipients. The idea of taking books that children love and packaging them in a fun, new way was finding its audience.

Susannah creates themed baskets of books, tailored to age and gender. For example, if a customer needs a gift for a boy who loves things with wheels, Susannah will create a basket of books that focuses on cars, trucks, and the like, and package the books in a Radio Flyer wagon. The Enchanted Bookery ships book collections all over the world. Now that Susannah's kids are older she decided to take on a partner to expand her clientele and her corporate client base. By chance, a longtime customer and mom who lived nearby was looking for a new venture. "Lynne was a big fan of The Enchanted Bookery so it was a perfect match." With more experience with social media, Lynne was the perfect addition to the company. And Susannah needed help if she was going to pursue the corporate market, which consisted of small to mid-size companies that needed gifts for their employees.

Susannah and Lynne are constantly researching to keep up with new trends and are always looking for books that children will love. Moving into the online world in 2001, Susannah created a website for The Enchanted Bookery. Social media has become a big part of their sales strategy.

When asked when their high season is, Susannah says, "There are new babies all year long, so we are always busy. I love that I have created my own business and can run it from home." Clients can pick their own book theme or choose from several baskets with a focus found on the site; with books, the sky is the limit.

If you have an idea for a product or service to make moms' lives easier or more fun, follow the lead of the women in this chapter. Who knows where things may go?

———

And if you have an idea for a children's class, you'll find several stories of inspiration in the next chapter.

seventeen

Creative Classes for Kids

Whether it's a manners class, sports coaching, or college counseling, there's a long list of services that children need and parents are willing to pay for. If you love working with kids and have a special talent or skill that meets their needs—either individually or in groups—you may have the basis of a venture.

CHILDREN'S CLASSES VENTURE PATH

In creating a class for children, your path might go like this:

- Test your idea with the target age group—and with their mothers.
- Formalize the process with supplies and timing to ensure smooth delivery.
- Name, brand, price, and market your venture.

If you choose to offer classes in your home, insurance may be necessary. Speak with your home insurance provider. Even if you offer classes at a different location, have each attendee sign an entrance form that includes a release of liability. Gather forms from other children's service ventures to know what to include in yours. Speak with other providers to know what else may be necessary.

If you're teaching a class that can be offered as an afterschool program or at a local library where you are simply acting as a teacher and being paid for your services, chances are you won't need additional insurance. Ask the institution offering the class what coverage is necessary (if any).

If you're opening your own studio, meeting the requirements will be your responsibility. Do your research to figure out what you need.

For many moms, offering classes for children requires no training. But these moms have a talent for wrangling kids and structuring and running an activity. If you do too—and wrangling kids is no mean feat—this may be where you'll find your passion.

CHILDREN'S CLASSES SUCCESS STORIES

Many moms not only found a service venture for children profitable, but also found a way to keep their own kids with them during their classes or while delivering a service. See how these four moms took talents from their life before kids and turned it into a venture for their kids and others.

Lovely Manners: Jill Ciporin

Having grown up in the South, she was a firm believer in the importance of proper etiquette. But Jill Ciporin never dreamed she'd be the one teaching others the intricacies of good manners. Starting her career in television at CNN, Jill became an associate producer of a morning show in Atlanta. Then her husband's job took them to New York and the family settled in the suburbs.

Once her two boys were launched into grade school, Jill began to think about going back to work. While reading an article about the importance of manners, she wondered why there wasn't a class available locally to give kids the basics of etiquette. "I'd love something structured for my two boys, and I thought I might be the one to teach a class." But she knew she needed some credentials and started her research. Her husband got involved and gave her the gift of a three-day Emily Post seminar. "It was a big investment and I never sign up for workshops like this, but my husband wanted me to pursue this venture." So off she went.

After obtaining her certification, she developed a fun format and curriculum to offer fifth and sixth graders the basics of etiquette. Her goal was to teach not only table manners but also other social skills including greetings, correspondence, and elevator etiquette. To hone her skills, she started with some practice classes with groups of neighborhood kids. Once she felt confident with her format she reached out to schools to get her first paying students. Offering her program as an afterschool class, Jill has found that many times Parents Association will pay her fee. The class is made up of three 1-hour sessions at $125 per child.

There was a huge interest in her class; for one offering, over 60 kids signed up. Clearly she had struck a chord and identified an unmet need in her community.

Jill put another spin on her manners program as well. Several years earlier, Jill's mother had created a placemat that showed children where eating utensils go and what they are used for. Jill wanted to bring this learning placemat back to the marketplace, but wanted to give it a modern feel. To do this, she accessed some manufacturing connections of her father's who helped her figure out how to create a green, U.S.-made product out of waterproof paper. A friend connected her with a graphic design student at Pratt who helped design the mat. Jill got input again from her neighbors and friends' kids to develop the final product. The mats can now be found in several locations in Jill's community and online. Each student in her class gets a free set of six mats.

Jill's current goal is to offer her etiquette class in more venues. Adding a blog is on her list of things to do, too. Who among us can't use more tips on using good manners?

JAM SONO: Dre Towey

Dre Towey's journey began in New York City, where she taught at an all-boys school and studied art education at Parsons. After taking a few years off when children prompted a move to the suburbs, she began teaching again, this time an art class at a local community center.

Throughout her life, Dre's creative side always dominated, and her own children inspired her. While she was teaching, she started writing stories for kids. When asked to illustrate a friend's songs, Dre jumped at the opportunity and not only did the drawings for her friend, but also turned her own stories into music. She picked up a guitar and took her first lesson while pregnant with her second child. These lessons marked the beginning of Dre's career as a performer.

Dre enjoyed success with her music group, Sugar on Top, and made her mark as both a recording artist and live performer. She had never dreamed of combining her love of teaching art with her music, but one day, while driving by a commercial space for rent in South Norwalk, Connecticut, the opportunity presented itself. When she first walked into the space, she thought, "I have to try." Dre used her savings, some of which came from record sales, to rent the space and outfit it for children's classes.

With a name that says it all, Junior Art and Music (JAM) was born. Offering fun in a hands-on, nurturing environment where judgment is left at the door, JAM is a one-of-a-kind studio that seeks to inspire budding artists and their parents. There are mommy and me classes for younger kids and drop-off art classes for older kids. The studio also has open studio classes offering a space for young artists to pursue their craft. Birthday parties are a big hit at the studio on Saturdays and Sundays. The website outlines all the offerings, details, and prices.

JAM's mission to allow children to tap into their creative side. Dre says, "Every child that walks in is inspired to create; they realize they can go in any direction they want."

Dre says her three children, ages 7, 10, and 12, have a love/hate relationship with mom's new venture, but her husband is her number one fan. "It's incredibly challenging to be there for them and run a business at the same time, but I know they are proud. I immersed myself in what I love and found I was personally more productive as an artist." The cool vibe found at JAM makes everyone want to get messy, create something new, and sing along with Dre.

Early Career Launch, LLC: Mary Bloomer

How do you translate a career in investment banking into a part-time venture when you have three kids and need balance in your life? On a whim, Mary Bloomer interviewed for a full-time position in the Career Development Office at the Yale School of Management, advising MBA students and alumni on their career plans. Mary felt the interview was the worst interview of her life (she'd been out of the workforce for 10 years, this was her first interview, and she told the team she'd need flexible hours). This was comical, considering that she was interviewing to advise others on how to interview. But as a Wall Street veteran Mary had the real-world experience the career development team was looking for, and they offered her the job.

The job was an hour away and it wasn't a financially compelling opportunity after hiring several hands to keep the household operating, look after and drive her kids, and walk her dogs, but Mary found she was good at leading new graduates in the right direction.

But it soon became clear that the flexibility that she was looking for would not evolve, so Mary left the position with great experience and a new passion for helping young people entering the workforce. She continued to work with many of the students on her own and this gave her an idea: "Why not start my own career counseling service, so I can create the flexibility I need in my life?"

After her recent experience Mary felt well qualified to start her company, Early Career Launch LLC. She contracted with two other colleagues she had worked with at Yale to create a team with experience across a wide range of sectors including financial services, consulting, health care, marketing, government, and real estate.

Early Career Launch offers career counseling services and a jump-start program for recent or soon-to-be college grads during the Christmas break. Mary works with students to help them define areas of interest, research opportunities, develop polished resumés, prepare cover letters, and hone interview skills.

Early Career Launch discusses options with potential clients in a free 30-minute assessment. The team then recommends a course of action and discusses prices. By providing a high-quality, individualized service to an ever-changing target market, the firm has experienced high demand.

Mary feels that putting herself back into the workforce in a new area that provided excellent training was a critical first step to creating a new venture. "With even the sharpest kids, I find areas to add value. On a personal level, I feel very lucky to have found something so rewarding and something that gives me the ability to be independent."

The Cookie Workshop: Carrie Memmesheimer

After attending a birthday party for her nieces where the seven-year-old guests got to make and decorate their own cookies, she thought, "What a great idea." Carrie Memmesheimer had been laid off from her job at a human resources company, and the idea of a something along the lines of a cookie-making party had been percolating in the back of her mind for some time. She would often bake with her own children and they loved the process. But starting a business around making cookies seemed like a scary proposition. So Carrie did what she always did when she started on a project—she got some help.

Reaching out to the Connecticut Small Business Development Office for guidance, Carrie was assigned a coach who gave her direction in putting together the numbers. She initially thought about offering cookie-baking workshops at home but then decided to go bigger—in the form of a cookie factory. "When I get an idea, I go forward. I'm not a procrastinator. I set schedules and deadlines and push through to get it done." She and her coach worked to bring her idea to life.

Carrie knew that this was a venture that would need funding if she was to offer the cookie-baking workshops in a location other than her home. Realizing that she didn't need a high-traffic storefront, she saved on rent and looked into buying a building that she could build out herself with a commercial kitchen. Her mentors through the Connecticut Small Business Development Office helped her with the logistics of this big project. Because her location was a bit out of the way, Carrie would make the store a destination for clients. She named her new venture The Cookie Workshop.

With her husband helping with the finances, she researched loan pricing for kitchen equipment and other start-up costs and found that a home equity loan was the least expensive form of funding. Carrie says having the strong support of her husband Rob was critical: "He was one hundred percent on board."

Now it was time for the fun part. Carrie created four flavors of nut-free cookie dough: chocolate, vanilla, strawberry, and chocolate chip. She offered cookie-making parties for kids from ages three to sixteen, as well as Mom's Night Out get-togethers—parties where guests get to roll out the dough for a complete batch of cookies and use more than 200 shapes of cookie cutters. All of her parties are theme-based, where the paper products and cookie decorations match the theme.

Carrie wanted kids to be able to see the baking process, so she built her space with a glass-enclosed kitchen in the middle. The children can watch the cookies bake and while they're waiting, they adorn the box they'll carry their creations home in. Once the cookies are done, the decorating begins.

Everything Carrie uses is made on the premises with no preservatives, and the kitchen and recipes are scrupulously nut-free. They also offer a variety of dairy-free, egg-free, and gluten-free cookies and cupcakes so kids and adults with these allergies can feel safe to celebrate with their friends.

Another idea Carrie offers is stop-by baking, "So you don't have to have a party planned to come by with a few kids and make cookies on an afternoon." Schools often bring in groups as a reward for special achievements. Aprons and chef hats are available to give young bakers the whole experience.

Carrie also offers preordered cookies and cupcakes, available with just a couple of hours' notice. They come in all varieties and can be gluten-free and dairy-free by request. The Cookie Workshop also sells cookie dough online available for pickup or shipping.

"Having my own business feels great. It's a lot of stressful hours and it was so scary in the beginning, but I know I'm building something for me and my family."

Take your idea for a children's class, do your research, and you too can be in business.

If your interests lie in fashion, and you like making, styling, or designing clothing or accessories for yourself or others, you may be enticed into starting your own fashion venture after you read about the stylish women in the next chapter.

eighteen

Fashion-Forward Ventures

Many creative moms out there make, style, or design clothing or accessories for their own use, only to find that others notice what they've done and ask them to make or do the same thing for them. Before long they realize they have a product or service that they can sell. If your passion to create something beautiful and memorable to wear—or help others to do the same—is as strong as your drive to have your own venture, work through the first 12 chapters of this book and get started.

FASHION VENTURE PATH

If you think a fashion venture may be right for you, here's what you must do:

- Decide if something you make and wear yourself, or a fashion-related skill you've developed, is something others would pay to have or use.
- Develop a name, branding, and pricing for your product or service.
- Start by selling to family and friends.
- Schedule a trunk show or showcase at a fair or holiday boutique.
- Reach out to local boutiques to place on consignment.
- Attend a large gift or accessory show.

If you have success selling to family and friends, move on to trunk shows. You would seek out one held by a friend or contact in a different town, allowing you to reach a new audience. Often small stores will have trunk shows, giving you an opportunity to display your items to staff (before selling to the public) or directly to customers for sale. They may ask for a percent of sales. Get clarity on this up front.

Many organizations have "boutiques" around the holidays and Mother's Day, where multiple vendors display and sell their products and services. At these events, you can rent a table to showcase your venture at a minimal cost and reach your target market. Ask in advance about how many people are expected to attend to make sure it's worthwhile. Create an attractive table with tablecloths in your brand colors and with effective signage. Offering treats for people who stop by to see your items is a good business practice. Be sure to ask for email accounts so you can follow up with this using your blog or newsletter.

Then move on to small stores. Some will only take your things on consignment rather than purchasing them outright. If this is the case, be sure to keep organized files on where your inventory is placed. Check back on a regular basis and if possible, work up to wholesaling your items to these stores or larger shops.

The next stop is to showcase your brand at major gift or fashion accessory shows, which take place a couple of times a year in major cities. This usually requires a large investment (typically between $2,000 and $7,000), and you'll want to make sure there's a demand for your item before going down this path. It might make sense to attend one of these shows before you commit to being a vendor to make sure it's a good fit and the right venue for your product. And be aware that if you get picked up by a large store or chain of stores you will be asked to deliver in bulk. Are you ready to mass-produce in the numbers they will be asking for?

Most moms with a venture in fashion start out selling in local boutiques and then move on to larger venues and even department stores, with those sales garnered through gift shows. Brands like Tara Michelle (swim coverups) (Chapter 5) and White Moth Jewelry (Chapter 10) can be found all over the country. Like so many moms profiled in this book, they had no idea where they'd end up when they started.

While many fashion ventures are created around a product, there are scores of others created around a service. Whether it's styling someone for a specific event or organizing a client's closet or helping with personal shopping, there are many ideas for creating a venture around fashion.

FASHION SUCCESS STORIES

Here are the paths four moms took to create their fashion brands.

In2Design: Inger Louise Baldwin and Inger Mark

What happens when two Swedish moms share a love of jewelry? Louise and Inger met while teaching in a Swedish afterschool program. Louise worked with her parents' importing business and Inger had been in hotel management. But when talking about all things Swedish, the two discovered they shared a love for a lariat necklace they had seen in their home country. Not finding that design in the states, they decided to offer their own, feeling they could put their unique spin on the style. The two formed a partnership on a handshake one afternoon after the class.

After sourcing beads, leather, and stringing, they began creating their line of lariats. They would work on necklaces out of Tupperware bins sitting on the sidelines at their children's soccer games. Other moms saw their creations and wanted to purchase them for themselves. Louise and Inger knew they had something special. So they took several pieces to a local store and got their first bulk order.

Shortly after that first order, they took a risk and invested the funds to attend a trade show. "I was at the Town Hall registering our LLC for the show and needed a name. Louise is my middle name; Inger is my first. I called Inger and she suggested Inger Times Two or In2Design. We figured we could always change it, but it stuck," says Louise.

At that trade show they sold to over 60 retail stores and were on their way. They got help from another mom, Louise's sister-in-law Christine, who handles the invoicing and orders for larger stores from her home in Massachusetts. Louise and Inger have a helper for assembly, another mom in Connecticut. Their creative Swedish lariat line has grown to include shorter necklaces and bracelets. Clearly, there is a demand for their unique pieces with their target audience of fashion-conscious women. The lariat has been a trend for several years. In2Design is now in over 500 stores nationwide and in the Caribbean.

What do they love about having their own business? Inger says, "We can still go to our kids' soccer games and have the flexibility we want in our lives." Louise says, "The entrepreneurial example we are setting for our kids is great." She wouldn't be surprised if one of her four children strikes out on their own after seeing how their business has succeeded. "It's always a balancing act between work and family but it's all worth it"— especially when they saw the Queen of Sweden wearing one of their designs.

Swanky Belts: Nancy Zlystra

Frustrated that she couldn't find the right belt buckle for a particular outfit, she took an antique brooch and used semiprecious stones to transform it into a belt buckle. Nancy Zylstra had worked for a fashion company before she had children, but she never planned to start a belt venture. However, the feedback from friends was so positive when she wore her belt that she visited a local store simply looking for input. She was instantly told, "Get your order pad out!" With this validation, Nancy geared up with supplies and began making more buckles with different adornments. She quickly realized she could create a business. She came up with a name, logo, and more samples, and she hit the pavement. Nancy visited local boutiques; six stores ordered 12 to 15 belts each.

She realized she would need to source the straps of the belts as well since stores wanted a complete product to sell. Nancy found her supplier online and is able to buy in the smaller quantities that she requires. Offering various colors and materials in the straps provides another profit center too.

At this point, Nancy needed a workroom. The loft above her garage was it. The Ping-Pong table became her work table and distribution area. She says, "It was wonderful having a home office where I could sneak off to, early in the morning with a cup of coffee before my family woke up or while my children were finishing their homework in the evening, and get a few buckles made and orders organized." Her husband and daughters joined in, helping her pack and deliver her belts to area stores.

When customers wore her belts on vacation to various destinations, the belts drew attention, and soon store owners from New York to Florida were calling. Client models and word of mouth spread the news about her designs. At her first New York City trade accessory show in the spring of 2009, she got orders from several stores and from the Ritz Carlton chain, which bought inventory for its hotel boutiques located all over the country and the world.

Realizing she needed more help and more space, Nancy secured a workspace close to home and hired another mom to help her fulfill orders. And then another big order came her way. In 2010, Calypso, a chain of popular boutiques around the country, ordered belts for 16 locations. She hired more help and looked for moms as employees since they work around their kids' schedules, as she does.

Nancy thinks of her belts as "jewelry for your waist." In multiple colors and layered adornments ranging from crosses to shells to graphic designs, she ensures there is something for everyone. "I love that I have created my own business using my background in fashion; that part is very fulfilling," Nancy says.

"The hero of my belt has always been the buckle," she says, but believes it's important to continue to evolve and grow. Nancy has added more styles of buckles, as well as handbags and leather jewelry with adornments such as pearls and gold beads to complement the belts. The latest season has brought several new belts based on an equestrian theme.

What does her family think? "They love the excitement my business generates in the house. I have two daughters, ages 17 and 20, who love the belts and even ask me to design certain styles for them. It's great in-house feedback."

Itty Bitty Bag Company: Jennifer Saint Jean

On the day her older daughter went to kindergarten, she quit her job. Jennifer Saint Jean had a big career on Wall Street, but when she thought about all she would miss with her girls, then ages five and one, she left to be a stay-at-home mom. While her girls kept her busy, she didn't like to be idle when she wasn't occupied with them and their activities. After about a month, she started her own business.

Always a seamstress, she had learned her skills from her mom when she was a child. Jen decided to make bridesmaid bags for a friend's wedding. The bags were just big enough to hold a phone and a lip gloss—they were itty bitty. After posting her creations on her Facebook page to share, she got requests for the itty bitty bags from friends, and a business was born.

Jen opened a bank account and an LLC and named her company after her bag—The Itty Bitty Bag Company. She used Etsy, the marketplace for handmade products, as her online store. That was in April 2009 and she hasn't looked back. Following the Etsy requirement that all products must be handmade and nothing can be manufactured or mass produced, Jen makes all of her bags herself, even hand-stitching the monograms.

Now she offers more than just the bridesmaid bag, even though custom bridal orders are the biggest component of her business. Jen will work with customers to choose the lining, the fabric, and the monogram to suit their tastes. The Itty Bitty Bag Company carries totes and bags in all shapes, sizes, and colors. One of the most popular bags she frequently offers is a medium size bag that she calls the "mom bag." "It's perfect for a day planner and an iPad."

Most of her sales come through Etsy, although some specialty stores do carry her bags. "I like knowing where all of my bags go. When I place my bags in a boutique, I don't meet the buyer of my creation. I lose the connection when I give my bags to someone else to sell."

Using social media to promote her business, Jen says building and maintaining relationships and marketing take up 50 percent of her time. She maintains an active blog, a Facebook page, and a Twitter feed. Thinking about the future, Jen may get help with manufacturing if she decides to increase her boutique business, but for now she's happy with the size of her business and her time commitment. How does the income from her business compare with what she was earning before? "Not even close, but salary isn't everything, and there are many other benefits."

What's the best part? Jen says, "I haven't given up me and I get to be a big part of my girls' lives. It's an amazing feeling that what I put into my business, I get out of it."

Wardrobe Stylist: Maria Turkel

What does the former costume supervisor for the hit show *Friends* do for her own venture? Maria Turkel went to school for fashion design and art history, then spent ten years working on television shows and movies in Hollywood. "For *Friends* I had to know each character's personality and background. Then I would shop the department stores, Rodeo Drive, and thrift shops to find what would work for them and their scenes."

A move back East with a new baby kept Maria out of the workforce for seven years, but when the youngest of her three children went to pre-school, she had an idea for her own business. "I wanted to be a personal stylist, helping people pull together outfits for all of the occasions in their lives. My husband said that if someone would pay me to do that, then go for it."

Maria got started with business cards and a simple website that de-scribed her service and listed her contact information. Then she told ev-eryone she knew about her venture. A local mom became Maria's first client. "It was a great feeling to get paid for my talent. I told my friends and soon I had four clients."

How does Maria work? "I usually start with a new client by doing a complete closet clean-out. We weed through what works, donate what doesn't, and organize what's left." Maria is skilled at ascertaining a client's personal style, and she works to showcase that. "The last thing I want to do is dress someone in clothes they don't feel good in. My goal is to high-light a person's true personality with the clothes they have plus a few of my suggestions. I want to help them be authentic while looking the best that they can."

Maria lays out outfits that include tops, bottoms, a handbag, jewelry, and shoes. She works to give her clients outfits for each part of their lives, whether it's work, everyday activities, a ladies lunch, or a night out. Maria often shops the thrift shops and antique malls for special pieces that might work for particular clients and outfits.

Maria makes her clients look great by using her knowledge of color, proportion, and composition. One client says, "After working with Maria, I received so many compliments on my wardrobe from my friends and family. She really helped me complete my outfits with accessories. I go to the 'Look Book' she created for me almost every day." The Look Book is a book of photos of the outfits Maria has created from a client's closet. Each outfit includes notes of the items that complete the look.

Maria charges $120 an hour for closet cleaning, wardrobe building, packing, special occasion dressing, and her other services. A Look Book is included in most of these services.

Maria also helps many clients on a seasonal basis, coming once a quar-ter to see what's needed to update a wardrobe. "Purge, purchase, combine—each season," is her recommendation for keeping a wardrobe current. She's also been able to help cancer patients who may have special wardrobe needs. She was happy to say that "One husband was so grateful that I was able to make his wife feel good about her new self after surgery."

"This is so much fun. I love the satisfaction of using my talents and having the flexibility to make my own schedule." She currently has between 50 and 60 clients who reach out to her for help. What does her husband say now? "He's so supportive and says, 'Keep going babe.'" And she will.

Like these women, you can take your fashion-focused product or service and build a venture.

————

In the next chapter, we'll look at the opportunities for building a venture around home décor.

nineteen

Ventures in Home Décor

M oms and homes go together, so what better place to look for a business idea than around your home? While you may not be a decorator, there are many good choices for business ventures that you can create around home décor. Something as simple as arranging bookshelves can be a venture, as we saw with Carolyn Taylor and Taylor Home (Chapter 6), or as involved as designing and implementing landscaping, as Karen Hughan does with her venture Good Gardens (Chapter 7).

Take a look at what others in your area are providing to homeowners. Is there a kernel of an idea there in line with a product or service that you can provide? What aspects of your home are you always complimented on? What do you do well at home? It could be something as simple as choosing paint colors or as involved as overseeing a renovation. See what area homeowners are paying to have done, then put your own spin and stamp on a venture.

HOME DÉCOR VENTURE PATH

A typical home décor path might look like this:

- If you have an idea for a product or service that can be used for maintaining or decorating a home, explore the possibilities for developing a venture.

- Research other ventures that provide a similar service or product for ideas and information.
- Market your venture to homeowners in your area or beyond (if your product or service can be delivered or provided online).

There are so many things that homeowners need to keep house. You just need to figure out what you can provide. Maybe you offer a service like staging homes for sale, acting as a property manager, planting gardens each year, or decorating for the holidays. Or you have a unique home product like one mom who makes metal mirrors, another who crafts glass coffee tables, or another who sews elegant and fun pillows. The ideas for home décor are endless.

HOME DÉCOR SUCCESS STORIES

Two home décor ideas that we've already read about are the service venture Smart Playrooms (Chapter 1) and the product Stick Storage (Chapter 5). The success stories of the three moms below will surely get your creative juices flowing.

Flourish Design and Style (design boards by email): Sarah Swanson

Working for a retail furniture store, she loved home design, but when Canadian Sarah Swanson had kids, she had to make a choice. Her husband had his own business as an ice hockey coach and Sarah went to work with him so she could have more flexibility. But she felt something was missing, "I didn't have a real connection to what I was doing."

After spending a great deal of time perusing design blogs, Sarah decided to take the plunge. So, in 2009, she began without a plan in mind. She started with one of the blog providers and learned as she went along. "I gained readers and the blog was an evolution as I learned more about the mechanics of how to use social media," she says. "I spent a lot of time on other people's blogs submitting comments. I had to put myself out there." This is how her followers grew.

Still working with her husband, in her spare time Sarah continued with her blog, Flourish Design and Style (now also the name of her website), but didn't produce any income. "But it was a great outlet for my creative design side." In 2010, she moved forward, deciding to offer to design via email, by providing a product mood board for the room a client wanted to redecorate. (A mood board is a page with items that would evoke a certain mood in a room. For example, for a family room with a boating theme, the mood board might include nautical items like rope bookends and sailboat prints.)

Her idea took off. Sarah begins with a questionnaire that covers style, budget, existing furniture, and family lifestyle. She has the client email a photo of the room they need help with, photos of rooms they like, and photos of specific things they love. She set her price at around $235 for a living room and less for smaller projects.

Then the fun begins. Sarah is very good at grasping a person's style and will keep revising the board until the client says "Wow. I love it." But she says, "I usually hit the mark on the first or second pass." She provides links to products at various price points (furniture, rugs, accessories) that the client can then order online. She'll also make suggestions for reusing large pieces that a client wants to keep. "I'm very good at working within a budget. Design boards are a cost-effective way to get design advice." This is like a Pinterest board designed for a client's specific needs.

If clients don't need a whole mood board but have a question about where to source a particular item or need advice on a paint color, they can get an answer for $10 on Sarah's website. Her girls, ages six and four, think what mom does—designing remotely—is very cool. "I never dreamed my blog would lead to this. I now do four or five boards a month and it's so much fun."

This is where things get interesting. Sarah's blog gave her the courage to start a full-service design business in her hometown of Calgary, offering the classic style that she had been showcasing online. Garnering design business through her blog, she was able to stop working for her husband and provide design boards and design advice full time. "It's a good feeling, doing what I love."

Leftover Luxuries: Wendi Smith

Sitting around a firepit sharing wine one night with her girlfriends, Wendi Smith started throwing business ideas around. With the new economic climate they talked about how everyone was reevaluating their spending.

As an interior designer, Wendi had leftovers from interior design clients. She also had evening gowns she'd worn once and clothes she hadn't worn at all, with the tags still on. Some of the women wanted to redo things in their homes but had no budget. Wendi came up with the idea of a group consignment sale.

Wendi says, "I always have leftovers from my clients—fabric, furniture, pillows, lighting, etc. Clients, friends, and I really started to think twice before replacing something that was in great condition, or we were less likely to just give things away. But, if I could sell what I wanted to replace and put that money toward purchasing new items, how sweet would that be?" From that came the name and concept of Leftover Luxuries. Wendi didn't want a storefront that would take a major part of her day to staff and manage and would also involve a large financial commitment. With two sons to manage, holding a large tag sale event several times a year gave her the flexibility she needed so she could set her own schedule around her boys' schedules. Since she lived in Charlottesville, Virginia, and had friends in different parts of the country, the idea of being mobile took hold.

Leftover Luxuries developed into a pop-up consignment shop in different cities where Wendi has friends who can help and who bring in both items and shoppers. The pieces that are consigned are generally listed at 50 to 75 percent off the retail price. Wendi's concept of providing a high-end sale took shape. People can sign up as consignees to sell home décor items. The consignee keeps 60 percent; Leftover Luxuries keeps 40 percent and provides the rented venue space, advertising, and promotional material to help bring in potential buyers.

As a mobile shop, Wendi works with contacts two to three months in advance to scout a location and to spread the word to friends in the area. Local people, designers, and retailers are all welcome to participate, but items must be approved by Wendi first. Leftover Luxuries focuses on furniture and home accessories with a secondary focus on personal designer and vintage items—clothing, handbags, shoes, accessories, and more— new or gently used. "The best part is setting up vignettes with the things that come in; it's like speed decorating with the items that are consigned."

This venture has taken off, with each event bigger than the one before. Wendi now has several events each year throughout the country. It's very much like a movable eBay store for upscale items.

La Grange de Silvermine: Sybille Campbell

Deciding what to do with all the cool vintage furniture that she couldn't resist buying at estate sales led her to a venture. Sybille Campbell loved to collect 18th-century furniture reproductions. But she wanted to make this distinctive furniture look authentic. Her friend Anne-Laure, also from France, taught her how to strip and repaint to give the wood a rich patina. Then, using elegant fabric to recover the upholstery, the look was complete.

With a new house to furnish on a budget, tag sales became an obsession. Sybille found many outdated pieces that owners were practically giving away. The styles were great but the finishes were no longer in style. She refurbished these pieces and placed them in her home. When her friends saw the look she had created with her tag sale finds, they asked Sybille if she could give their furniture the same French-inspired feel or source unique items for their design needs.

Sybille says, "I realized there was a void in the market for fun and trendy vintage pieces and decided to start a business." She knew she could source things very inexpensively. Once she put her spin on the item and her labor into it, the value went up considerably.

Sybille set up a workshop and a showroom in her barn in the Silvermine section of New Canaan, Connecticut. While her two children are in school all day, she spends her time in the barn stripping and painting furniture. "I love the artistic side of what I do." Her first sale in the barn showcased this newly named venture, La Grange de Silvermine, and established Sybille's reputation as *the* source for vintage French-inspired furniture. Since then, Sybille has been busy gathering new items to refurbish and transform. Accessories, including pillows and lighting, are also collected, repaired, and offered in her showroom.

On top of her collection of furniture and home décor accessories, La Grange de Silvermine offers a unique form of pop art she calls "Syb'lhouette," another tribute to the 18th century. From a profile picture of the subject—kids, adults, pets, or objects—she creates a colorful silhouette, sometimes pairing the subject with another item. The final product can be printed on canvas, Plexiglas, metal, and pillows. These are custom-made for clients and add a personal element to a room's décor.

Sybille shows her work by appointment and stages several events open to the public throughout the year. She completes about 10 to 20 pieces of furniture a month, so the inventory changes frequently. Asked whether there have been pieces that are hard to part with, Sybille says, "There are some things that I don't want to sell; it's hard to see them leave the show-room, but this is my kick. I love to visualize something with refinished wood and new fabric. I'm very proud of each piece."

————

The next chapter explores how communication ventures can lead to success.

twenty

Say What You Want to Say: Publishing Ventures

Whether it's an idea for a book or an innovative way to track medical records, publishing ventures present great opportunities for moms who want to create and share ideas and information. Getting a book published can be an undertaking using the traditional route, but self-publishing has become a viable alternative. You can even print on demand now, which gives you flexibility in terms of ordering and inventory. Many women have developed successful ventures based on their own publications or products that make keeping and sharing information easier and more efficient.

Kelly Corrigan started with a book about her family and has continued in that vein. Samantha Walravens gathered essays from women about the choice between work and staying at home with children. Both these women followed the traditional route to getting their books published. Other moms have self-published. See all their stories below.

If you have a book idea, do your research and get feedback. Talk with friends or contacts who have published books to ascertain what the best approach is for you.

The subject of how to self-publish a book could fill a book itself, and you will need to do some research on the Web to see if it's the right path for you. David Carnoy has written an excellent article offering practical, realistic advice on everything you'll want to consider before taking the plunge into self-publishing. You can find it here: http://www.cnet.com/news/self-publishing-a-book-25-things-you-need-to-know/.

Identifying your goals is half the battle. Are you looking to go the traditional route with a known publisher or do you want to publish on demand and quickly? Are you just looking to publish a book for your followers or do you want to use the book to gather new clients? Many writers self-publish and their high sales garner the interest of a traditional publisher. All of these issues and more will come into play as you make your decision on how to present your work to the world.

BOOK PUBLISHING VENTURE PATH

Whether you publish or self-publish, whether your book is found in the bookstores or is an e-book, your journey will probably begin something like this:

* Share your book idea with friends and family to get feedback and encouragement.
* Research and join a local writers' group in your subject area.
* Talk with as many writers as you can in your genre to get feedback and gain knowledge.
* Research whether self-publishing is the right option for you.
* Draft a proposal including a description of your topic, summary of the book, table of contents, and a sample chapter. Send it to book agents who represent your genre.

A lot of research goes into not only writing a book but also getting it published. Look at books that are similar to what you'd be publishing and keep a list of the agents and publishers who publish these writers. Most agents have guidelines posted on their websites for submitting a proposal. Many would-be writers send their information to agents following these guidelines and then follow up with an email.

If you have a contact, use it. It always helps to know someone who can get your work seen.

BOOK SUCCESS STORIES

Many books have been written on the process of getting published, so whether you have written the whole thing or only a few pages, research the process and dive in. Learn how these moms orchestrated their success as writers.

Writer: Kelly Corrigan

Journaling since the seventh grade, Kelly Corrigan had always wanted to be a writer. "This was my dream, flat out." So when she was diagnosed with breast cancer at age 36 and at the same time found out her father had late-stage cancer, she decided to write about her experience. Kelly felt the pressure of taking care of both her children and her father while she herself was dealing with a serious illness. The record of her journey became her first book, *The Middle Place*. It's a memoir about taking care of herself with cancer in the middle of raising two young children and helping her father deal with his own cancer battle.

But how did she secure an agent and then a publisher in the competitive world of nonfiction? "My sister-in-law had a friend who had a friend, so I was three-degrees of separation from Andrea Barzvi [who became her agent]. Having a referral got Andy to take a look at my proposal. Turns out we believe in the same things, cry over the same things, stew over the same things, and want the same things." Barzvi signed her as a client and found her a publisher. She was on her way.

When her first book made it onto the *New York Times* Best Seller List in 2008, she became an author to watch; her dream of being a writer was coming true. So she wrote another book, *Lift,* which was published in 2010. It is written in the form of a letter to her children. It looks at a family in crisis through three different stories. Readers find the book deeply inspirational.

For further exposure, Kelly posted a reading of a paper called "Transcending," which became a YouTube favorite. With these books to her credit and a desire to reach a wider audience, Kelly signed with a speakers' bureau and has become a sought-after speaker. She thinks and writes a lot about the power of women: "I have strong feelings about what we are all capable of and what stops us from pursuing our true interests . . . What can we all do together? How can we use ourselves up? What should we be throwing ourselves at? What is worth our full attention? I want to round all of us up and get to work on something that really matters."

Kelly usually writes during the day while her kids are in school. She says of her work, "Writing is how I figure out what matters. I have these stories I have retained and I know there is a reason why the memories of those experiences have lasted while others have fallen away. If I keep writing, I think I might be able to unravel every last one.”

Writer: Sam Walravens

Torn between being home for her family and working 80 hours a week, Sam Walravens hit a wall one day. “After a horrific two-hour commute home along a backed-up freeway, I found myself in the kitchen screaming at my husband to make his own dinner while throwing a box of breakfast cereal on the table in front of our two-year-old son,” Sam remembers. She built a venture around this experience and the feelings it created.

With a master’s degree in English and women’s studies, Sam had moved to San Francisco to be with her fiancé and found work with *PC Magazine* as a journalist. “It was an exciting time to cover these amazing start-ups of Silicon Valley.” From there she took a position with a software company that was on track to go public. By now married with a son, Sam soon realized that with her huge job commitment and her husband traveling a lot of the time, the nanny was basically raising her child. She was expected to practically live at the office.

With a second child on the way, Sam was torn. She remembers thinking, “This is crazy. I’m a horrible mother and a terrible employee at the same time.” Her boss realized her heart wasn’t fully committed, so Sam went to a part-time status, which eventually led to not working at all. This left Sam feeling alone and alienated. “It was expected of my generation of mothers that being a mom was not enough. I felt I should be working.”

Six years later and the mother of four children, Sam started a conversation with friends, asking the question, how do you feel about being torn? Not surprisingly, moms were ready to talk about it and share their stories. And the stories were what intrigued Sam. She went one step further and posted a request for submissions responding to this dilemma on a message board at Princeton, her alma mater. Not surprisingly, replies came in from all over the country and from all walks of life.

The commonalities found in the trials of balancing work and motherhood were compelling. Sam was amazed at how remarkable and motivating the stories were. “With close to 100 submissions, each struggle touched me in a different way—some were sad, some were funny, all were real.” She knew she had the makings of a book and was driven to get it published.

Acting as editor, Sam compiled the stories. She sent out numerous proposals, and, after receiving 50 rejections, finally found an agent to represent her, who then sold her book to a publisher. This led to the publication of *TORN: True Stories of Kids, Career & the Conflict of Motherhood*. Never giving up on her goal to let women know there is no right or wrong way to be a mother, Sam now promotes the book through speeches around the country. What's next? Fathers wrote in, asking, "Where is the book with fathers' stories?" Perhaps that's Sam's next project. But for now she is very proud to have created a forum for mothers everywhere who are torn by competing demands.

Writers: Carolyn Dingman and Darcy Mayers

Who knew that a response to a blog post would lead to a book and a meaningful friendship? That's exactly what happened when two moms started responding to each other's blog posts and emailing each other outside of their blogs.

Darcy Mayers and Carolyn Dingman each had begun a blog about motherhood: *Post Picket Fence* (found at http://www.postpicket.blogspot.com/) and *Carolyn Online* (formerly found at http://carolynonline.blogspot.com/), respectively. Dealing with everyday life, the online essays covered motherhood, marriage, ill-fitting jeans, ill-fitting in-laws, booze, and the ever-persistent, nagging question "what now?" The blogs themselves were fulfilling ventures for both moms and allowed Darcy and Carolyn to vent and share the often hilarious, sometimes embarrassing, and many times meaningful stories of their lives with their kids and husbands. With five kids between them, their stories covered everything from diapers to tricycles to braces.

Finding each other online, through blog responses, the two moms created a modern pen-pal relationship. They say they have reinvented the coffee klatch with WiFi and are working to create a portrait of 21st-century womanhood shared through their blogs.

Blogging fit these moms' lifestyles perfectly; they could write anytime they had a free moment. Carolyn owned a small company that produced construction documents and Darcy worked at a record company called Midnight Feeding. All this fun came to an end when both women had kids and decided to stay at home. They needed an outlet to share their triumphs and agonies; blogging came to the rescue. "No training needed," as Darcy says. "This is pretty much an on-the-job training kind of thing."

Both women feel that aside from their friendship, they have preserved a slice of their lives to look back on and maybe share with their children. It has inspired Carolyn to write a novel—a dare from Darcy. Darcy feels that the experience has been nothing but awesome.

Taking it one step further, the women decided to publish their correspondence, which consisted of the barely edited emails between these moms who lived thousands of miles apart. In fact, they published their book before they ever met in person. *TO: A True Story in Letters* is made up of their blog posts and emails over the course of several years.

Darcy and Carolyn did some research and found a self-publisher, blurb. com. This company prints copies on demand and takes a cut of the purchase price; it also acts as an on-demand seller. The two women used their book to share their blog in another format and to build their followers. It also produced some income, never unwelcome.

PAPER PRODUCT VENTURE PATHS

Books are not the only things that get published. Greeting cards, specialized notebooks, individualized mementos, and more. Many women have created ventures around stationery for people who still believe in handwritten notes, for example. Other products present opportunities as well. Earlier you read about how Candice Frankel created a folder (The EDWIN) to help high school students prepare for college admissions (see Chapter 7). If you have an idea for a paper product, the steps below will show you how to get started.

- If you have a paper-based product in mind, do some research to determine if you can create a venture around it.
- Get feedback on the format from friends and family.
- Research pricing and packaging and determine how you'll present your product and to whom.
- Find a manufacturer to create your product if you can't create it yourself.

Paper products are not going out of style any time soon. While some believe that eventually they will go the way of mimeograph machines and phone booths, many feel they must see things on paper to have them be real. And other products are for older people who don't like things stored on a computer, like the Green Pear Health folder seen in the story below.

PAPER PRODUCT SUCCESS STORIES

Read the two stories here to learn how these moms created ventures around paper products.

Green Pear Health: Paula Rapp

When you're a nurse in the Emergency Room you experience firsthand what happens with a patient and family members in a dire situation. That's what Paula Rapp repeatedly witnessed over many years.

Paula was on the front lines when patients communicated with doctors and nurses in the ER. This led to an idea for a product. "So many people, particularly elderly patients, come in without any idea of what their health history entails," Paula says, "They don't know what medications they are taking or in what dosages. Some patients come in with a bag of empty pill bottles for the ER nurses to decipher, while others request that their doctors, pharmacies, or family members be called to retrieve vital information. And so often they arrived in the ER after regular business hours, when no one can be reached."

Many of these patients are also equally confused as to their diagnosis or even the names of all their treating physicians. "When minutes can be critical, hospital personnel may not have the time to play detective. And even when we can get a family member on the phone, they are not sure about the current medications." Paula's idea was to create an organizational health binder that would contain all of the pertinent health information needed by everyone as they age. Her nursing background gave Paula the knowledge of what needed to be in the binder.

Why not put this information on a computer or the Internet? "Most people want to be able to grab a hard-copy binder and head to the ER. A key fact too is that the elderly are usually not as tech savvy as younger people. And an adult child of an elderly parent can keep a copy of the binder and keep it up to date and call in if they are in a different location."

Paula says, "Sitting in triage and seeing patients overwhelmed by their own health history led me to create my product. My most obvious target market is the older generation that generally has the more complicated health history." Paula believes the binders serve to enhance the healthcare experience for everyone—the provider, the patient, and the loved ones.

Wanting a name for her company that reflected an eco-friendly focus, Paula chose Green Pear Health. A mom from one of her children's playgroups assisted with graphic design and Paula was ready to go. Paula sourced a binder manufacturer that could create what she envisioned. "Coming up with my binder format was easy, but I had no business experience."

Paula researched business training opportunities that her community offered and found a three-month class offered by the Women's Business Development Center. The class helped with the learning curve for running a business. Paula set up an e-commerce site, which she manages in between raising her two boys. Paula's marketing strategy is to spread the word on her product through health fairs and related venues. She created additional logs that can be added to the binders, including specific diseases, advanced directives, symptoms, and nutritional tracking.

Green Pear Health is a direct outgrowth of what Paula was doing in her career, and she feels great about helping patients and their loved ones organize and simplify the medical part of their lives.

Jumbo Dog Art Books: Jessica Anderson and Yael van Hulst

Two moms are standing in the street after their kids get on the bus. One mom says, "So what's on for your day?" The other mom says, "Walking the dog, going to the grocery, and mopping the floor . . . a very exciting day." When Yael suggested the idea of a business creating art books out of children's past art projects, Jessica jumped at the prospect. These moms had left jobs in the city when they moved to the suburbs, at first going part time, and then leaving work altogether.

Both women wanted to work but lamented, "Who will hire someone who needs to be home by three, takes days off when the kids are sick, and needs school breaks off?" They figured they'd have to work for themselves. When they came up with the idea of the children's art books, it seemed like the perfect venture. Extremely excited, Jessica dove into the research.

Their idea was to create books that would be pieces of art themselves. Yael says, "So many parents these days collect their children's art and it ends up in a bin or bag in the closet and they don't want to throw it away.

We thought it would be great for people to have a coffee table–quality book to display and have forever."

They knew they would need a wide-format scanner for artwork and photo equipment for the "pinch pots" and other things like masks that kids create in their art classes. So with a major investment up front, the two women got organized.

They needed a name. Yael's bulldog Jumbo seemed like the perfect place to start. With Yael drawing a cartoon of Jumbo, the logo took shape, and Jumbo Dog Art Books was born. Creating books for themselves with their own children's art, they tested several suppliers.

Jessica and Yael chose a provider that could deliver the kind of product they wanted to offer, with rigid pages and high-quality photographic silver halide paper. Seeing one of their books you know there is value in the creative vision these two women see in your child's artwork. Jumbo Dog offers two kinds of books: a stunning book with a glass cover and a leather back, and a beautiful hardcover book featuring a single image that wraps entirely around it.

Working together came naturally. "It was very collaborative and we each had a different skill set. Yael takes care of the finances and I work on the marketing." So how do the logistics work? They pick up the art, scan or photograph the pieces, design the books, and then send a proof of the book to the client before placing the order. Clients have three options as far as book size, and four options for number of pages.

Books get made for celebrations, sporting events, and as special gifts. They even take photos of actual things like trophies to include in some books. The women plan to scale up by offering their books nationwide. One client said when she got the finished product, "I don't think words can describe how wonderful this is. It literally brought tears to my eyes." Another said, "I am in *tears* . . . this book is so beautiful, so special, and just amazing! The girls are so excited about this surprise for Daddy . . . and I am too!" Making something that families will treasure—that's a good idea for a venture.

In the next chapter you'll read about how several successful ventures in art were launched.

twenty-one

Your Art, Your Venture

Many women succeed at balancing life with kids while creating a business venture around their art. Often their work gets noticed by friends and family, who then want something created for their own homes. When this happens, it's an opportunity to build a business. You've been given the validation to go to the next level and make art a venture.

Before you put your creations on the market, you'll want to look at what is selling in your area and for how much. Price your work accordingly. Talk with local design shops and decorators to get a feel for how your work will be received. These two groups can be a source of sales. Keep lists of these groups so you can update them on your progress and notify them of any art shows you're entering and any new works in process. Set up a website that includes an artist's statement. This tells the user what motivates you and talks about the esthetic you are trying to create with your work. Look at what other artists put on their sites and get ideas from them.

VENTURE PATH FOR ARTISTS

The path for artists often follows the one outlined below:

- If you're an artist and your work has been appreciated by friends and family, you may be able to create a venture based on your art.

- Offer to loan your art at no charge to local shops. Make sure your contact information is available.
- Price and promote your pieces to local design and gift shops on consignment.
- Enter local art shows and fairs.
- Build a list of followers to stay in touch with.

You must be proactive about getting your work into the public eye. Whether a loan to a local bank or shop or an offer to supply art for an office building, at the beginning you may need to let others borrow your work so it will be seen. Make sure to oversee the handling of your art and that you put cards with your contact information by each piece.

Enter local art shows and fairs and be on hand to answer any questions about your work. Create a portfolio of all that you do, and showcase each piece and the room in which it hangs. Include these items on your website.

ARTISTS' SUCCESS STORIES

See how the women in the following stories created an income-producing business with their art. Also, look back to Lynne Byrne's success story in Chapter 6.

Wall Candy Arts: Allison Krongard

Appreciating her design sense from her work with a modern-style furniture company, friends asked her to help decorate their kids' rooms. Allison Krongard had a strong modern esthetic and wanted to use large graphics and murals on the walls. She did a lot of research but couldn't find the kinds of stick-on wall appliqués that she wanted. Stenciling was not an option, and painted murals cost a fortune and would be impractical to change as a child's interests changed. She looked for a product and couldn't find it. Suddenly she realized that if it wasn't available in the marketplace, maybe she could be the one to offer it.

She felt she had a great idea and it was worth taking a chance. Selling her apartment to raise funds, Allison quit her job of nine years in sales at Knoll Furniture and went all in. At this point she was single, with no children, and felt it was the time to take a risk. She spent a year attending conventions to learn about the adhesives industry and develop her product. "My first step was to license designs from Marimekko to create the large wall art."

Allison created a temporary adhesive product that was nontoxic. It was a high-quality vinyl that could be easily applied and removed without damaging the walls. She began with themes of all sorts including birds, butterflies, and flowers; elephants, dogs, and cats; buildings, cars, and boats; popsicles, clouds, and rainbows—the design ideas were endless. Allison named her newly formed business Wall Candy Arts.

In the beginning she was asked to work with her friend's son on his room. The child loved meeting with her and she treated him like a real client. The mom even called and told her, "You cannot cancel; my son has been planning his meeting with you for days." Allison realized how important it is for a child to be involved in the creation of their environment and her wall art was instrumental to that end.

With her first run of five designs, she placed an order for 2,000 pieces. She had garnered a commitment from a design store in New Canaan, Connecticut, so she was confident enough to take a chance on a large order. Turning her apartment into a central shipping base, on many days Allison could be seen pushing a large cart of boxes down the streets of Manhattan to the UPS mailing store. She marketed her Wall Candy Arts to kids' design stores. Her orders increased. After two years, Allison turned to a warehouse in Virginia that could ship her product more easily.

Allison handled her own press, using the Internet to get contact information for the editors of regional newspapers around the country and sent them her story. "It was a grassroots effort that paid off." One of her goals is to scale her business, and Allison is working with a few well-known designers and licensing their designs into wall art. She's now branching beyond kids into teens, young adults, and even adult decals. Allison invented peel-and-stick chalkboard wallpaper and holds a patent on the product. Now a mother of young children, Allison explained, "My three-year-old was writing on the walls with chalk and I thought it would be cool if there was an adhesive chalkboard."

Allison says, "The best thing about having my own company is that I get to go to my kids' school events. I make my own schedule . . . I like to be in charge of my own destiny. The harder I work the more I make." With her product now in over 2,000 stores worldwide and with two kids ages five and seven, she feels the gamble was worth it. It felt like a huge leap of faith eleven years ago, but when you see the Wall Candy Art used in the windows of Barneys in New York City, you know she was right to roll the dice.

Artist: Laura Trask

Sometimes your outlet for happiness can lead to a venture. That's what happened when Laura Trask started painting. With a degree in fine arts and a past career in interior design, Laura had always been interested in art, but she never thought it would be a career. When looking for something to do just for herself she began painting and it grew into a passion.

As her body of work grew, Laura took her pieces out into the world. "I started with small cafés, asking them to showcase my work, and this led to commissions and other venues. When my first piece sold, I knew I had found my life outside of motherhood." Laura has two girls ages 16 and 10 who are very proud of mom's talent and brag about her all the time. She says her work makes people smile.

And she's not just a painter. Laura loves to repurpose old furniture by repainting it. She's not from the South but her esthetic evokes a bit of a Southern vintage flair with a Northern attitude.

Laura takes commissions for her work, and one of her most popular is a word search on a large canvas. "I hide words that are meaningful to the family buying the piece. Hung in a family room, it becomes an art puzzle of sorts for family and friends to solve."

Laura had been asked to place several works in a local art show, and at the end of the show she told the organizer that her goal was one day to be a featured artist in the show. Two years later, while shopping at Party City, she ran into that woman. Within a week she was asked to be featured at the Community Cooperative Nursery School (CCNS) Art Show in Rowayton, Connecticut. "It was an amazing experience." The CCNS Art Show has been called a "boot camp for artists." And it was. Laura says that after this experience she saw her venture from a true business perspective.

Laura was able to create a studio by redoing her garage. "I even put in an intercom to the house. This was a mistake because as soon as I would get ready to put brush to canvas, my kids would call for something." Laura says balancing kids and a full career as an artist can be tricky, but she loves creating. "I can't imagine my life without this; it's what makes me happy and sane."

Artist: Charlotte Sabbagh

The vistas she saw in her native country of Denmark inspired her to paint. Charlotte Sabbagh had always been creative and loved design. Working as a project manager on the interiors of the high-end W Hotel in Honolulu, Charlotte says, "I saw the way art can complete the look of a space."

In search of classical training, Charlotte went to school and received her degree in fine arts from Parsons in New York. She took classes while her children, twin boys and a daughter, were young. She began to paint and create pieces for her own home. Then she had a moment that changed everything—she put her house on the market. The real estate brokers who came in to preview the house loved her art and wanted to buy it. She thought, "Why not?" and her hobby turned into a business practically overnight. She sold her paintings to brokers and their friends, and news of her work spread by word of mouth.

When she had a designer come in to help with choices for her new home, she got the same reaction. "She asked to feature my work in the storefront of her showroom." Now Charlotte was on her way in a big way. "I got several commissions from that exposure and from other designers." Charlotte even placed her work in local art shows.

What makes her work popular with clients? "When I'm commissioned to do a piece, I meet the client in their home and get to know them. I work to create something that resonates not only with their style of living but more importantly with their personality, while at the same time using my esthetic."

Charlotte feels it's important from a business perspective to keep her finger on the pulse of current design trends, particularly color and texture. She works to incorporate those trends into her art. Her Scandinavian background brings a modern element to her style.

To further her sales, Charlotte reached out to and secured several corporate clients and has been commissioned to create a series of works for offices, lobbies, and hallways of buildings. "This is becoming a big part of my business," she says.

Charlotte always knew she had a creative side, but when she expressed it through her soothing landscapes, she was able to bring it to life. "I love when people appreciate my work. It makes me happy to share my vision with others."

IN CLOSING

Congratulations! You made it. You've thought about what you really love to do, you've done your research, you've gotten feedback from family and friends, and you've created a brand. You now have your own business to focus on and take to the next level. I so appreciate that you took this journey with me, and I sincerely hope that this book has helped you get your start-up started. Remember, your circle of friends and family will help you immensely and they'll be there when you stumble and when you succeed. Rely on them.

If there is any final message I'd like you to take away, it's that you are a powerful person, and you can do anything that you set your mind to if you are authentic to who you are, passionate about what you do, and persistent in your efforts.

And here's a favorite quote that keeps me going:

Twenty years from now you will be more disappointed in the things that you didn't do than by the ones you did. So throw off the bowlines. Sail away from the safe harbor. Catch the trade winds in your sails. Explore. Dream. Discover.
—Author unknown

All the best in your new venture,

RESOURCES

Logo Services

LogoMaker: logomaker.com
99designs: 99designs.com/logo-design
FlamingText.com: flamingtext.com
GraphicSprings: graphicsprings.com
DesignMantic: designmantic.com
COLOURlovers: colourlovers.com
LogoVictory.com: logovictory.com
LogoYes: logoyes.com
SloganMania: sloganmania.com

Email Marketing Services

Constant Contact: constantcontact.com
MailChimp: mailchimp.com
VerticalResponse: verticalresponse.com
iContact: icontact.com
Litmus Scope: litmus.com/scope/
Premailer: premailer.dialect.ca
AWeber: aweber.com
Campaigner: campaigner.com

Emma: myemma.com
GetResponse: getresponse.com

Stock Photos

iStock: istockphoto.com
Dreamstime: dreamstime.com
Shutterstock: shutterstock.com
Depositphotos: depositphotos.com
Can Stock Photo: canstockphoto.com
Bigstock: bigstockphoto.com

Tag Lines

Tagline Guru: taglineguru.com
Strategic Name Development: namedevelopment.com/tagline-development
Slogan Mania: sloganmania.com/tagline-development
Slogan4u: slogan4u.com

Website Development

WordPress: wordpress.com
Weebly: weebly.com
Squarespace: squarespace.com
Wix: wix.com
uCcoz Web Services: ucoz.com
Yola: yola.com
Website.com Solutions website.com
Virb: virb.com
Moonfruit: moonfruit.com
Websiteworks: websiteworks.com

Social Networking

Facebook: facebook.com
Twitter: twitter.com
Pinterest: pinterest.com

Instagram: instagram.com
LinkedIn: linkedin.com
Google: plus.google.com
Meetup: meetup.com

Blogging

Blogger: blogger.com
WordPress: wordpress.com
Create Blog: createblog.com
squarespace.com: squarespace.com
Thoughts.com: thoughts.com

Small Business Resources

Small Business Administration: www.sba.
SCORE Association: www.score.org
National Association of Women Business Owners: nawbo.org
National Women's Business Council: www.nwbc.gov

INDEX